FLYING PRECISION MANEUVERS IN LIGHT AIRPLANES

FLYING PRECISION MANEUVERS IN LIGHT AIRPLANES

RON FOWLER

ILLUSTRATIONS BY JAN AVIS

PHOTOGRAPHS BY JOHN TATE

DELACORTE PRESS / ELEANOR FRIEDE

Published by
Delacorte Press/Eleanor Friede
1 Dag Hammarskjold Plaza
New York, N.Y. 10017

Manufactured in the United States of America
First printing
Designed by Oksana Kushnir

LIBRARY OF CONGRESS CATALOGING IN PUBLICATION DATA

Fowler, Ron.
    Flying precision maneuvers in light airplanes.

    1. Airplanes—Piloting. I. Title.
TL710.F65   629.132′520422   80–17274
ISBN 0–440–02598–2

This book is for Mary Blackwell,
for whom teaching people to fly safely
was the most important thing in her life.

ACKNOWLEDGMENTS

The ideas of a good many people are included in this book. The facts and procedures that appear within the text are, to a large extent, reflections of my associations with fellow flight instructors, examiners, pilots, and students (from whom an instructor learns more than the student ever realizes).

There is no way to acknowledge individually everyone whose ideas are contained here; however, each can easily recognize his own contribution as it appears in the book. And he can take satisfaction in knowing that his ideas are being passed along for other pilots to use.

There are a few contributors, however, who must be named. Ed Karvonen (FAA, retired) has for many years provided the standard against which his instructors can measure their own performance. So much of his teaching has gone into this book that there is scarcely a page that does not benefit from his influence.

Mary Blackwell achieved excellence in her own performance, and managed to let those around her know that she felt them capable of the same high degree of accomplishment. She was both flight instructor and designated examiner. Many of the discussions she and I enjoyed over the years have found their way into this book.

Betsy, my oldest daughter, is a grammarian at heart. Her efforts with the manuscript of a pilot-turned-writer have assured you a readable text. My wife, Helen, typed, retyped, and re-retyped the manuscript—a formidable job in itself. But of greater significance, she provided good-humored encouragement throughout our entire task. Actually, the magnitude of this contribution can be fully appreciated only by those of you who have themselves set out to write a book.

My sincere thanks to all the many contributors.

Ron Fowler
Orlando,
Florida
May 1980

pre•ci•sion ma•neu•ver   1. *noun.* a drill in aircraft control that follows a predetermined flight path, that when flown precisely demonstrates the capability of the aircraft and proves the skill of the pilot.   2. *verb.*   to fly the aircraft exactly in accordance with the pilot's wishes; to follow an exact flight path; to attain or maintain predetermined airspeeds, altitudes, and headings; to manage control pressures and power settings in a safe and precise manner with exact timing.

—Author's definition

CONTENTS

Introduction   1

Precision Flying: The Basic and Special Considerations   9

1.

Steep 720-Degree Turns   31

2.

The Chandelle   51

3.

The Steep Spiral   73

4.

Lazy Eights   93

5.

Pylon Eights   115

6.

Precision Slow Flight   139

7.

Accuracy Landings   151

8.

Short-Field Landings   163

Conclusion: Precision in Every Flight   171

FLYING PRECISION MANEUVERS IN LIGHT AIRPLANES

INTRODUCTION

Correct . . . exact . . . precise! Is all that effort, all that discipline, necessary in our day-in, day-out flying? Yes, it is. Certainly. Aware pilots strive for perfection every moment that they are in an airplane. (We may not achieve perfection . . . but we constantly strive for it.) Because we *know* that when trouble climbs into the cockpit, real, meaningful help is *not* just 121.5 MHZ away. The only meaningful help lies within our own store of knowledge, judgment, and skill as pilots; any "Mayday" is best transmitted to the *reserve of competence* that lies deep within our own flying ability. Aware pilots know too that this reserve is acquired through hours of seeking perfection in their day-in, day-out flying.

Think of it this way: Picture yourself (riding in the rear seat) on two separate flights. The pilot of each plane holds a different attitude toward his own flying. The first is a pilot who strives for perfection with every landing. His patterns are correct . . . his approach speeds are precise . . . he selects his touchdown spot and makes it good, with no sidewise drift . . . and his roll-outs are straight down the centerline. The other pilot is content to land "somewhere on the first third of the runway." Now, let's put each of these pilots on a precip-laden instrument approach. And to put each pilot under a little pressure, let's have their soggy radios cut in and out. Then let's have each pilot break out at 300 feet on a too-short final, wide of centerline and a trifle too fast, to find a 20-knot wind gusting across the rain-slick runway—at night. Which pilot has the better chance of landing safely? Which pilot has a *reserve of competence* . . . and which pilot would you rather be riding with? The daily quest for precision, then, builds and reinforces this store of skill and knowledge, this reserve.

But precision in our day-in, day-out flying is difficult to attain. Once attained, it is just as difficult to maintain. And for a sound and simple reason. Anytime we pursue perfection, however elusive, we are usually striving to-ward a clearly defined goal . . . a criterion with which to measure our performance. When we were working toward our pilot certificate, we were presented with many such goals. For instance, we had eventually to prove to our instructor that we could slow-fly the plane within set tolerances for altitude, airspeed, and heading.

But once we had earned our certificate, those very visible goals seemed to evaporate. Our training over, we relaxed and found ourselves lacking the motivation to seek perfection in our daily flying—simply because we had no new criteria to grade our flying against.

This book, then, provides a new set of goals . . . and a means of self-evaluation. Each chapter presents a high-performance or precision maneuver. Each maneuver develops and tests certain pilot skills that are essential to proficient everyday flying: airspeed control, coordination, timing, attitude control, orientation, and others upon which flying skill and safety depend.

Each maneuver is broken down into its *separate parts,* and it is shown how each part can stand on its own as a training drill. These separate parts are not really difficult to master, once you are able to recognize the visual clues that tell you when and how to handle your pitch, roll, and power at keypoints within the maneuver. And you will quickly discover how practicing each of these segments (which serves to polish a particular flight skill) develops precision in your daily flying. A part of the chandelle, for instance, shows just how torque affects your roll-out from a climbing left turn— knowledge you can apply to, say, improving your pattern exits.

Once the separate parts are mastered, I describe how to put them together for the complete precision maneuver, and how to grade your performance against tolerances given for airspeed, altitude, and heading.

Each chapter ends with a short summary of the maneuver and provides an in-flight practice guide for you to follow during in-flight practice sessions. The practice guide first reviews the techniques that the maneuver intends to develop. Sharpening these pilot skills is, after all, the prime reason for learning to fly precision maneuvers. The steep power turn, for example, develops and tests the pilot's ability to remain coordinated under conditions of high power settings and unusually heavy load factors.

The practice guide offers on-the-spot operational tips that will remind you of the visual aids to use and the pitfalls to avoid as you fly the maneuver.

The practice guide then identifies the *keypoints* of the maneuver—the critical moments when you must manage the plane's pitch, roll, and power with particular precision and finesse. Each loop of the lazy eight, for instance, contains five such keypoints.

Finally, the practice guide provides the means for grading your performance: the acceptable tolerances for airspeed, heading, and altitude for the maneuver.

In-flight demonstration is, of course, an integral part of flight instruction. The drawings and photographs are presented with this in mind. The line drawings trace the flight paths of the maneuver so that you will carry a picture of the entire maneuver pattern to your in-flight practice. The drawings also identify the keypoints throughout the maneuver.

Completing the in-flight "experience," the photographs show a pilot's-eye view of the visual references seen from the cockpit at these same keypoints. The visual clues help develop precise control and timing at these critical points.

Earlier I attempted to define "precision maneuver." But the term conjures up concepts difficult to define to the satisfaction of all pilots. Once you are in the air, precision flying becomes more of an idea than an exact procedure . . . an idea or concept that will vary slightly from pilot to pilot, as each strives to master the maneuver. Your own idea of precision flying may center around words like challenge, discipline, self-satisfaction —and this is valid.

Precision maneuvers are not as spectacular as airshow maneuvers. But mastery of these demands just as much effort and devotion as the airshow stunts do. And once a pilot trying to master precision maneuvers accepts self-imposed discipline, he finds a potent competitor and challenger—himself.

Self-improvement and honest self-evaluation of our flying skills is never an easy task. We become poor disciplinarians and tend to be too lenient with ourselves. We're prone to forgive our mistakes or sloppy flying with a halfhearted promise to do better next time. But the satisfactory performance of a precision maneuver does not allow for leniency. Each must be gauged against precise standards. In flying the chandelle, for example, the pilot must apply pitch, roll, and power in proper sequence and magnitude, with precise and predetermined timing. If all of this is not done, the pilot must give his maneuver another name, for it is not a chandelle.

The average pilot will need a lot of self-discipline and concentrated effort for his precision maneuvers to meet accepted standards. While certainly within the grasp of the average pilot, they are not easy. He must lift his skills *above* average to master any one of them. (And a pilot who can fly these maneuvers within these tolerances is indeed qualified to begin aerobatic training.) Most pilots will not be able to fly a maneuver satisfactorily in a single session and will need at least two or three flights devoted to each. So try to fly at least once a week for an hour's session, and confine each flight to a single maneuver.

But let me say this: If your flying skills—any aspect of them—appear to have eroded to the point where you feel unsure, even uncomfortable, with your airplane in your normal flying, it's clear that you are due for some dual instruction. In this event, I urge you to take and heed at least an hour's instruction in each of these precision maneuvers prior to beginning your in-flight practice.

We are all entitled to satisfaction anytime we test our potential and win. Without a doubt you'll deserve and enjoy that satisfaction after you've mastered these maneuvers. You'll enjoy, too, occasionally taking the plane up to fly through the symmetry of a perfectly executed lazy eight or the tightly knit, fast action of skillfully flown pylon eights. But the greatest reward will probably come one day with the realization that you have achieved the same degree of skill and precision in your everyday flying—and, should the situation demand, knowing that you will be ready with your own backup system, your reserve of competence.

PRECISION FLYING: THE BASIC AND SPECIAL CONSIDERATIONS

Airplanes have operating limits. The flying you have done up to this time may not have taken you and your machine very close to these limits—but they are very real. Allow the speed in your dive to pass through red line, and the aircraft manufacturer suddenly loses interest in his warranty. Put stresses on your plane that the designer did not anticipate, and you invent a new flying machine—with you aboard as test pilot. Spin accidentally for the first time, solo, and you immediately enter a do-or-die, on-the-job training program.

When you are flying precision maneuvers in light,

nonaerobatic airplanes, background theory—the basics —becomes *practical* information. And "practical" is a good word to describe the way we discuss theory in this chapter. It is meant to be used in the cockpit as you fly the maneuver.

You must take special safety precautions before and during your practice sessions, because each drill presents new challenges to your pilot skills. You use your total effort to master each in turn. And once you enter the maneuver, much of your attention is normally centered on the plane and its flight path. You can become so preoccupied that a midair with unseen traffic is possible, or you can run out of altitude and luck at the same time. The fighter pilot calls this preoccupation "target fascination." Psychologists call it "fixation." But whatever label we give it, the results can be disastrous unless we take special precautions *before* we become enmeshed in the maneuver's demands.

THE BASIC CONSIDERATIONS

Load Factors   An airplane seems to change weight through centrifugal force anytime you change its flight path. (As a kid, did you ever swing a bucket of water around you by turning rapidly roundabout? Centrifugal force kept the water from pouring out of the tipped bucket. Your arm also told you that the bucket of water felt much heavier in its turning flight path.) We call this apparent gain in weight the load factor. If the total weight doubles, we refer to the load factor as 2 G's—twice the weight of gravity.

Angle of bank determines the load forces imposed on your airplane (Figure 1). The plane you fly is designed to withstand a certain maximum load factor: Aircraft rated in the *normal category* are stressed to withstand a load factor of 3.8 G's; *utility category* airplanes withstand 4.4 G's. (Cherokees and Mooneys are examples of normal-category aircraft; Cessna 152's and Sundowners are examples of utility-category aircraft.) The engineer quietly sitting at his drafting table calls these critical stress limits "yield factors." A pilot sitting at the controls, however, calls this "where my plane may bend and buckle." Before you take to the air, check the Operating Limitations section of your plane's operating manual (or owner's manual) for the category that applies to your airplane, and confirm the allowable load factors.

Figure 1 shows that the allowable load factor for a normal-category aircraft (3.8 G's) occurs in a coordinated, *level* 73-degree banked turn. A utility aircraft (4.4 G's) reaches its stress limit at a 76-degree bank. In some precision maneuvers you hold altitude in a 50-degree bank, near the edge of the plane's operating limits. What do you do if your attitude indicator nears the critical bank?

1. Lower the nose slightly (reduce back pressure) to immediately relieve some stress.
2. Simultaneously reduce power to prevent an increase in airspeed.
3. Reduce your angle of bank.

LOAD FACTOR

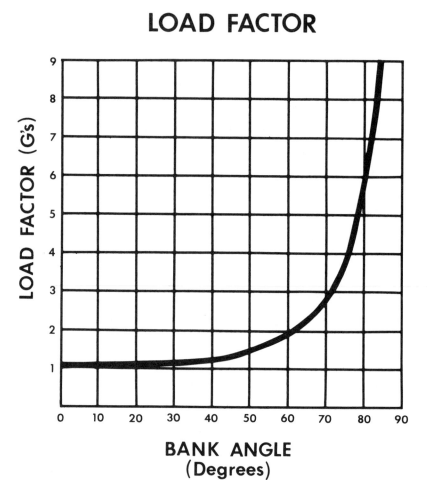

Figure 1
Load factors in a coordinated *level* turn.

Load factors adversely affect stall speed: *Stall speed increases in direct proportion to the square root of the load factor.* Thus the 75-degree bank that produces a 4.0 load factor (the square root of 4 is 2) doubles the stall speed. Stall speed increases 150 percent in a 63-degree bank—only slightly steeper than the 50-degree bank called for in some precision maneuvers.

You can cause a high-speed stall through abrupt and large control deflections and impose dangerously heavy loads on your airplane. It's possible to yank the wheel hard enough in a steep turn or a pull-up to stall at *twice* your normal stalling speed and put a 4.0 load on your plane—enough to do some damage.

To prevent this, each plane has a designated *maneuvering speed:* the maximum speed at which you can use abrupt control travel without exceeding the design load factor. Or stated another way: Maneuvering speed is the maximum speed at which you can stall the airplane and not risk damaging it. This speed is also given in the Operating Limitations section of your airplane's manual. To calculate it yourself, multiply your plane's normal stalling speed by 1.95 (the square root of 3.8) for "normal" category, or 2.1 (the square root of 4.4) for utility aircraft. The result very nearly equals the manual maneuvering speed.

(Normal stalling speed here means flaps up, gear retracted, wings level, and idle power. This speed is denoted as V_{s1} and is shown as a *calibrated* value at the bottom of the green arc on your airspeed indicator. V_{so} is another significant power-off stall speed: Wings level, flaps and gear extended—in landing configuration. You will find it at the bottom of the white arc on your airspeed indicator.)

However you arrive at it, maneuvering speed is critical to the safety of precision maneuvers—enough so that you might want to print it on a 3 by 5 card and tape it to your instrument panel. Your homemade placard will remind you to use smooth control pressures if you exceed maneuvering speed.

Some precision maneuvers (steep turn, chandelle, lazy eight, pylon eights) are conducive to over-control. If you become disoriented during these exercises, it is possible for you inadvertently to control too briskly and force a high-speed stall. If you fly a high-performance airplane (such as a Mooney, Centurion, or Bonanza), modify the airspeeds specified in the in-flight practice guide and substitute your plane's *maneuvering speed* for the specified *cruise speed*—simply use the slower of the two. (A Mooney's cruise speed of 170 knots greatly exceeds its maneuvering speed of 135 knots.) If you fly a low- or medium-performance plane, such as a Cessna 152, Cherokee, Skyhawk, Arrow, or others, you will find that maneuvering speed equals or exceeds cruise speed. In these cases, of course, you may enter the maneuver at cruise speed. In any event, study the Operating Limitations section of your aircraft's flight manual. Modify the stated in-flight practice guide speeds so that you do not exceed your aircraft's maneuvering speed.

Never-Exceed Speed (Red Line)   The never-exceed speed is the maximum speed at which you can dive or glide your plane and not risk loss of control or structural damage; it is marked on your airspeed indicator as a red line.

Never-exceed speed is determined by the designer through practical tests, and a small safety margin is added. This margin, however, was adequate only when the plane was new—before the rigors of age, corrosion, hard landings, and turbulence took their toll. Red line is an unforgiving operating limitation.

Should you find your diving plane getting close to the red mark, take immediate action:

1. Reduce power to prevent further acceleration.
2. Level the wings to reduce stress on your plane as you *slowly* raise the nose to reduce your speed.

You of course raise your nose slowly to avoid abrupt control travel. But this slow recovery to level flight results in a considerable loss of altitude, so make sure your working altitude allows for an inadvertent dive and recovery. The minimum working altitudes in the in-flight practice guides are predicated on a low- or medium-performance plane; if yours is a high-performance retractable-gear airplane, adjust the stated altitudes upward by 30 percent.

Stalls and Spins   Before you start flying precision maneuvers, take to the air for a review of stall recognition and stall recoveries. Some maneuvers take you close to stalling speed with high-load conditions, and an accidental stall is very possible. Only recent practice in stall-recovery technique renders them harmless. And recent practice in stall recognition allows you to fly out of an impending stall before it fully develops.

Many pilots shy away from practicing stalls and stall recoveries. Often this is a holdover from student-pilot days. Almost universally this stems from the pilot's exaggerated mental image of the plane's attitude at the point of stall. Hand a model airplane to a student pilot and ask him to show what he thinks the stall attitude looks like. Invariably the student demonstrates a 45- to 60-degree pitch attitude (Figure 3). Of course, the actual pitch attitude in a power-off stall is only about 15 degrees relative to the horizon. Power-on stalls are about 7 degrees higher.

The student's erroneous and worrisome concept of the stall attitude leads him to two conclusions—also wrong—regarding the airplane's behavior when it stalls. He thinks the plane either slides downhill, tail first, or that it flops over on its back. (Actually, the plane settles about 20 feet—trying to land—then pitches forward.) Incidentally, the student visualizes an exaggerated pitch angle because he keeps his eyes straight ahead during the approach to the stall. The view out beyond the nose reveals only empty sky, and this viewpoint can make it look as though the plane is pointed nearly straight up. If the student would only look left or right at his wing tip against the horizon, he would see the true picture. To see for yourself what the actual stall attitude looks like, go to the airport and look at a parked tail-wheel airplane—*that* is the stall attitude.

The best drill for practicing stall recognition is to fly for several minutes at minimum controllable airspeed.

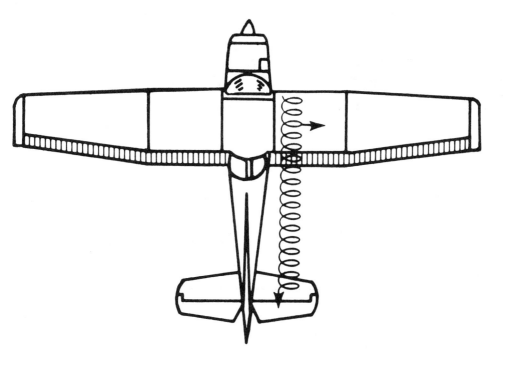

Figure 2
An airplane gives three warnings of an impending stall.
    1. The stall warning indicator winks or beeps.
    2. The ailerons seem loose and unresponsive.
    3. The plane "buffets."
The stall warning indicator is designed to activate 5 to 8 knots before the wing completely stalls. Begin each inflight practice session with an operational test of your plane's stall warning indicator.

A wing is designed so that the wing tip stalls *after* the wing root has stalled. This minimizes the plane's tendency to roll out of control at the point of stall. The feeling of unresponsiveness in the ailerons is due largely to the reduced airflow passing over them and tells the pilot that the wing is about to stall.

The plane buffets when the wing root stalls and the disturbed airflow tumbles rearward and shakes the horizontal stabilizer. This produces the buffeting that warns the pilot that the stall has started and is working its way out to the wing tip.

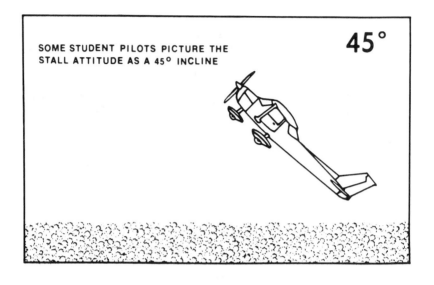

SOME STUDENT PILOTS PICTURE THE
STALL ATTITUDE AS A 45° INCLINE

45°

A 15° INCLINE IS NEARER THE TRUTH

15°

Figure 3
If you shy away from practicing stall recoveries, this is probably due
to a misconception held over from your student pilot days.

Minimum controllable airspeed means that if pitch is increased or roll (and load factor) is increased without additional power, a stall develops. Easily recognized in the cockpit, minimum controllable airspeed keeps the stall warning device sounding. Practice shallow turns, climbs, and climbing turns. Lower your nose for a recovery anytime you feel the buffeting or loss of aileron control that warns of an impending stall.

Since a stall is possible during a precision maneuver, so is a spin—a spin evolves from a stall. For your own safety and confidence, it is essential that you log some dual in spin recognition and recovery before you tackle solo practice. Do not attempt to teach yourself spins. (This would be as foolhardy as a two-hour student pilot teaching himself landings.) While spin recovery technique differs from plane to plane, they all seek the same end results. The recovery must: 1. stop the rotation. 2. break the stall. 3. minimize the loss of altitude. With some aircraft, the pilot can stop the spin's rotation by merely neutralizing the rudder. Other planes call for full opposite rudder, a few require the pilot to hold opposite rudder for 2 or 3 additional revolutions before the rotation will stop.

Stick pressures needed to break the stall vary from merely releasing back pressure; to forward pressure; to *full* forward stick travel. Every make and model has its own best procedure for stopping the spin in the least amount of altitude lost. Many aircraft owner's manuals spell out the manufacturer's recommended spin recovery—but some do not. And some cover the stall recovery only in general or vague terms. Rather than try to interpret your aircraft manual's spin recovery technique, seek out and practice with an instructor who is familiar with the spin characteristics of the plane you intend to use.

You may have to interview several instructors before you find one to give you instruction in spin recognition and recovery. Not all instructors teach spins. And not all schools want their planes spun. (Those nontumbling gyros *will* tumble in a spin, and they are expensive to fix.) Take the time to find a willing and able instructor with a suitable plane.

The plane you actually use in your maneuvers may be placarded against *intentional* spins. Nevertheless, get the training—but in the right aircraft. Then have the instructor review with you any variations in spin recovery that your plane demands.

The Region of Reverse Command   As it pertains to precision maneuvers, the region of reverse command (or, as it's also called, "the back side of the power curve") describes the plane's climb performance at certain airspeeds. Your plane gains its maximum altitude for each unit of time at its best-rate-of-climb speed. (As opposed to best-angle-of-climb speed that produces the maximum altitude for each unit of distance.) If you pitch your plane upward for a speed lower than best-rate-of-climb, climb performance suffers. You are approaching the region of reverse command.

Picture yourself flying a 100-horsepowered airplane

straight and level at a cruise speed of 90 knots (104 MPH), at 2400 RPM. To maintain altitude and slow your plane to 80 knots (92 MPH), you reduce your power to 2200 RPM and slightly raise the nose. A further reduction to 70 knots (81 MPH) calls for a further power reduction (say 2000 RPM), and a slightly higher nose. Another speed reduction to 60 knots (70 MPH) requires another power reduction (to about 1800 RPM) and more nose-up pitch. But if you make a final speed reduction to 50 knots (58 MPH), it suddenly takes *additional* power to maintain your altitude. You need more power to fly slower and still maintain the desired altitude; you are flying in the region of reverse command. At best, your plane has only minimal climb performance at this slow speed. This is so because your plane's climb performance at any *particular airspeed* depends on the power it has available, additional to that needed to maintain altitude at *that* particular airspeed. Another example of flying in reverse command: Imagine yourself cruising level in the same airplane at its top speed of 100 knots (115 MPH), with *full* power. How much climb performance does that plane have at 100 knots? None. It needs all available power just to hold altitude at that top speed. Now imagine yourself in that same plane, staggering along, nose high, at 45 knots (52 MPH), with *full* power needed just to keep it in the air. How much climb performance does the plane have at this minimum speed? Again, none. The plane needs everything the engine can give, just to hang in the air. Obviously, somewhere between the plane's maximum and minimum speeds lies an optimum climb speed, and this is the best-rate-of-climb speed.

Torque   In precision maneuvers, especially, a plane is subjected to several forces we group together and call "torque." We combine them because they work together to produce similar detrimental effects:

1. Torque creates a *left-turning tendency* anytime power exceeds cruise power and airspeed is less than cruise speed (takeoff runs and climbs, for example).
2. The *absence* of any torque force often creates a *right-turning tendency* when power is less than cruise power (as in a glide).

Torque consists of four separate forces:

1. True torque
2. Slipstream effect
3. P-factor
4. Gyroscopic precession

Torque tends to produce a twisting motion to the plane. The propeller, in turning right (viewed from the cockpit), tries to twist the plane to the left. The designer compensates for this left-turning tendency, and the plane is rigged to counter this effect at *cruise speed and cruise power.* But if you exceed cruise power, the built-in torque compensation is not adequate. You must hold right rudder to prevent a left turn. Descend with a lower power setting, on the other hand, and the built-in compensation overcorrects—your plane tends to turn right.

Slipstream effect is caused by the propwash. The downward-swinging blade in the right-hand half of the propeller arc pushes the air under the fuselage. This slipstream then corkscrews up around the left side of the plane and flows upward to strike the left side of the

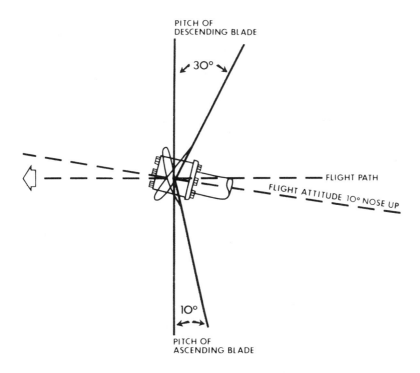

Figure 4
P-factor is produced when you pitch a plane upward. The blade in the right half of the propeller arc has a high angle of attack and develops more pull than the left half of the propeller arc. The plane tends to turn left.

vertical stabilizer. This, of course, tends to turn the plane to the left. Slipstream effect is most apparent during the first seconds of takeoff run, right after full power is applied. Quick right rudder keeps the plane on the centerline.

P-factor is present only when the plane is pitched upward (as on lift-off). At this moment the blade in the right half of the propeller arc has a high angle of attack and develops more pull than the left half of the propeller arc (Figure 4). The plane tends to swing left.

Gyroscopic precession affects a tail-wheel plane as the pilot lifts the tail in preparation for lift-off. The propeller's motion creates a gyroscope. Since the spinning propeller is a gyro, the turning force of the uplifted tail acts as though it were applied from the right side. Again, the plane tends to turn left.

A THEORY OF LEARNING

The Building-Block Method   Here, precision maneuvers are taught in a "building-block" sequence. The mastery of each new maneuver depends upon the pilot skills developed in the preceding one. And each maneuver develops pilot skills necessary to fly successfully the one that follows. You will get more from your in-flight practice if you tackle the maneuvers in the order of presentation and begin in-flight practice of a maneuver only after you have mastered the previous one.

As you read along, you will see that I present a maneuver in a *what/why/how* format. First I show just *what* the maneuver is and what it involves. In discussing the chandelle, for example, you will learn that it is a maximum performance climbing 180-degree turn in which eight essential elements must be present. These are then discussed in detail.

You should also know *why* you should learn a particular maneuver, which pilot skills the maneuver is designed to develop, and how it helps develop these skills. Again, in the chandelle, you will see that three essential pilot skills are stressed, and why you must fly the maneuver in the prescribed manner.

A *whole-part-whole* concept is used for the *how* of each maneuver. The maneuver is first described in its entirety, with certain elements pointed out. Then the step-by-step discussion focuses on flying the individual parts of the maneuver, the difficulties you are likely to encounter, and how to avoid or remedy them. As with the chandelle I describe the eight separate parts of the maneuver, how the pilot should respond to each one in turn, and I point out common mistakes.

Finally, the text shows how these segments fit together to produce the whole maneuver.

What/Why/How; Whole-Part-Whole   These simple teaching formulas have served me quite well over the years. I think you will find them useful as you become your own flight instructor during your practice sessions.

THE SPECIAL CONSIDERATIONS

Preflight   As with every flight, a thorough preflight using the manufacturer's walk-around and cockpit inspection checklist is mandatory before attempting these precision maneuvers. You, as pilot, must preflight your own physical and mental condition. Are you really feeling up to par? Are you taking any stress or worries to the air? You and your machine must be in top shape, because these maneuvers demand maximum performance from both you and your plane.

Your Practice Area   There are several factors to consider when choosing a practice area—factors that help ensure a safe in-flight session. Basically, your practice area must satisfy an important condition surrounding your practice sessions: During inflight practice, much of your attention is devoted to the plane and the maneuver and, try as you will, you cannot keep an effective traffic watch while you fly through the intricacies of the drill. Only careful advance planning and special safety procedures can minimize the chances of a mid-air.

Choose a practice area at least 7 or 8 miles away from any busy airports. All too often an arriving pilot fixes his attention on his destination airport. Chances are that this pilot—involved with traffic, communications, setting up his approach—will not see your airplane. If the airport has an instrument runway, avoid any area lined up with that runway for a distance of 12 miles. You can expect high-speed instrument traffic turning final within this area, at about 4000 AGL and descending. Rightly or wrongly, the IFR pilot's attention is glued to his panel.

Avoid any practice area with an established airway running through it. The airways are highways in the sky, and that means heavy traffic. (All navaids, especially airways intersecting at VOR's, are crowded.)

Check your sectional chart to make sure you haven't chosen an area within or adjacent to a Restricted Area, Military Operations Area, Alert Area, or Intensive Military Training Area. These are well marked on your chart and pose obvious hazards.

Also check with the flight service station nearest your proposed practice area to make sure there are no VFR Low Altitude Training Routes nearby. The military fighters that fly this airspace travel in excess of 300 knots (when you see 'em, it's too late, and often they cannot see traffic).

Call on the experience of others. Ask a flight instructor at your airport for his advice.

Once in your practice area, do everything possible to protect yourself from unseen traffic; alert them to you. Fly with your landing light blazing away. You may not see head-on traffic, but he will certainly see you. By the same token, turn on your strobes if you have them. They are quite visible even during daylight. (A red rotating beacon, on the other hand, is of little value during the bright day. You usually see the plane before you see the beacon.)

Fly with your transponder on. Even though you are not in touch with a radar controller, he will see your blip and warn his traffic of your presence.

Consider choosing your working altitudes in 250-foot intervals (3250' or 3750' for example). Most pilots fly the 500-foot levels (3000' or 3500' for example). Choosing the odd altitudes avoids the heavier en route traffic.

Don't practice in low ceilings or visibilities. Low ceilings squash all VFR planes down into a narrow band of high-density traffic—just what you want to avoid. Low visibilities invite a midair. Today's planes travel fast. Two head-on planes flying 150 knots cover 3 miles in 36 seconds—simply not enough time for you to decide that the speck ahead of you is a plane (and not a flyspeck on the windshield), realize it presents a hazard to you, decide what you must do to avoid it, take action, and still have time for your plane to respond to your control. Practice when the ceiling exceeds 4000 feet and visibility is at least 7 miles.

Clean your windshield before you take to the air. Sunlight on a dusty windshield cuts visibility. Bug-smashes are hard to see through. And it's annoying to repeatedly take evasive action from a flyspeck. (Late in a session you may find yourself differentiating between single-engine flyspecks and multiengine flyspecks. Interpret this as a sign of fatigue and go home.)

Precede each maneuver entry with a pair of 90-degree clearing turns. Search out that band of sky 3 inches above and below the horizon and scan each sector of sky. Upon turning your head toward each sector, move your *eyes* rather than your head for an unblurred look. And remember that your eyes work like a telescope. You must vary your range of focus. We tend to focus only out to the horizon—and look right through a nearby plane.

If your practice area is floored by obstacles or ridges of significant elevation (1000 feet or more), you should of course modify the minimum working altitude for each maneuver and increase it by the elevation of the terrain or obstacles.

Knots Versus Miles per Hour   When describing the maneuvers, I discuss airspeeds in terms of knots rather than miles per hour. I personally do not favor one scale over the other. Knots were chosen simply because most of the newer airspeed indicators seem to favor them. But if you feel more comfortable with MPH than you do with knots—use them. And when I say "use a speed 5 knots greater than stall," simply treat it as "5 MPH greater than stall." While the difference is too small to worry about, equivalent MPH speeds are also given in parentheses in most instances using knots; use these if you prefer.

The important thing to remember about airspeeds as you work your way through the following precision maneuvers is this: Decide on the precise speed you want to fly—call your shot. Then *make* the plane fly exactly as you *want* it to fly.

STEEP 720-DEGREE TURNS

Steep 720-degree turns are consecutive left and right 720-degree turns (twice around each way) flown at a 50-degree bank. Good performance requires that you establish the bank smoothly and promptly and hold your desired altitude within a 100-foot tolerance during the entire sequence of entry, turns, crossover to the opposite turns, and recovery to straight and level. Controls and power should be precisely coordinated throughout the maneuver. Once into your 50-degree bank, do not let it vary more than 5 degrees. Recovery to level flight should be smooth, prompt, and on a heading within 10 degrees of the entry heading. That, basically, is the steep 720 turn.

This is a good maneuver to begin your precision flying. It is not complex, as it does not require simultaneous *and* continuous changes in pitch, roll, and power. Yet it will develop and test your ability to fly competently while you and your plane are subjected to extreme attitudes and high load factors. Specifically, the maneuver will polish the skills needed for control coordination and for geographic and aircraft orientation—all while those 50-degree banked wings are subjecting you and the plane to nearly 2 G's.

The steep 720 turn will teach you two basic facts. *First,* you cannot let an unfamiliar load factor confuse you . . . and with a little practice you'll learn to be quite comfortable with a load factor. (If the 50-degree bank causes you real discomfort, try a few practice turns at a milder 30- to 45-degree bank.) *Second,* with constant scan of *outside* references, you can fly oriented even when operating near the plane's performance limits.

Can the skills learned in the steep 720 turn be applied to everyday flying? Yes, very probably. Possibly one day on short final, low and slow . . . a quick turn to avoid a plane that is cutting in. Or the unexpected wake-turbulence that suddenly stands you on wing tip just over the numbers—or any other low-altitude maneuver that will not tolerate the loss of a single foot of altitude, knot of airspeed, or moment of confusion.

Steep 720's can only be described as exhilarating: bending the plane over into the left turn . . . hauling the nose twice around the horizon with the engine singing under climb power . . . the G's pressing you tight against the seat, allowing neither slip nor skid nor loss of altitude . . . the smooth roll into the right turn . . . and twice around again before rolling the wing level to recover to cruise.

Take it a step at a time. Before entry select an altitude at least 3000 AGL and align your plane with either a north-south or an east-west line on the ground. These ground references will help you stay geographically oriented throughout the maneuver. Frequently a pilot learning the steep turn will become too involved with the intricacies of the maneuver and fail to keep track of his path over the ground. If you tend to lose track of your position during the turns, simply announce aloud to yourself "west"—"south"—"east"—"north": each position as you cross it. (Most parts of the country offer a practice area floored by a patchwork of prominent north-south, east-west "section" lines. If your neck of the woods does not, a prominent, perpendicular road intersection will do.)

Plan your first few steep turns as 360-degree circuits, and in only one direction. Once you become familiar with the visual references and the feel of high load factors, the turn may be extended to 720 degrees. When you see what the full 720 degrees require of you, start working on the complete maneuver, with alternating consecutive left and right 720-degree turns.

This is an aggressive maneuver. In rolling into the first turn, you should have the full 50 degrees of bank established before you have flown through the first 45

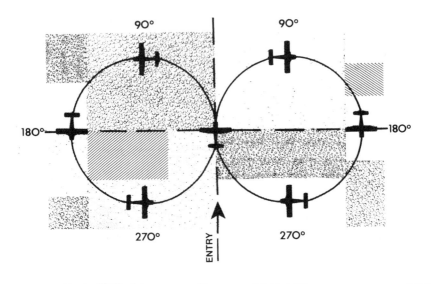

Figure 5
The Steep 720-Degree Turn
1. Use the north-south, east-west reference lines to determine your 90-, 180-, and 360-degree positions within the maneuver.
2. Roll left and establish 50 degrees of bank within 45 degrees of entry.
3. Add climb power as the angle of bank nears 50 degrees.
4. Apply back pressure to the stick as the wings hit 50 degrees of bank.
5. Cross-check the attitude indicator and ball to verify proper bank and coordination at each 90-degree point within the maneuver.
6. Fly through a left turn of 720-degrees duration and then roll immediately toward a right 720-degree steep turn.
7. Relax back pressure and reduce power as the wings pass through the level attitude during the crossover.
8. Reestablish back pressure and climb power as the angle of bank reaches 50 degrees in the right steep turn.
9. On recovery to entry heading, return pitch and power to normal cruise as wings level.

degrees of the turn. Some pilots initially feel uncomfortable with this rapid rate of roll. Their previous flying has rarely required this kind of aggressiveness, nor have they had to establish such an extreme attitude so quickly. It may take several attempts before you feel at home with the maneuver entry.

As your bank nears 50 degrees, increase back pressure and extra power at the correct time and in the correct amount, if the plane is to remain within 100 feet of entry altitude.

Pilots have difficulty establishing and maintaining the pitch required to hold altitude in steep turns because the bank is so steep and unfamiliar, and much more back pressure than they anticipated is needed. Moreover, a slightly higher reference point relative to the horizon, with which to gauge the necessary nose-up pitch, must be quickly determined. (Remember, if you are flying a side-by-side plane, your line of sight will not be straight over the nose. As I expect you are flying from the left side, the nose will *appear* higher in the left turn than in the right turn.) Until good outside references are learned, you can find the proper pitch attitude by scanning the vertical speed indicator with your peripheral vision while flying the first few practice turns. Another reason pilots have difficulty holding proper pitch involves a bit of psychology: Some pilots tend to lean away from the steep turn . . . a defensive move, I suppose. But doing so, of course, distorts outside references and renders them useless. You can't position your plane's nose properly against the horizon from a cockeyed viewpoint. If you find yourself leaning away from the turn, try this: Sit straight, hard against the back of the seat; *pilots invariably begin leaning to one side* only *after leaning forward.*

As your bank reaches 50 degrees and your plane gains the weight of the extra load factor, extra power is needed to hold altitude. Use a power setting appropriate to your plane. Full throttle is fine in low-powered trainers, such as a Cessna 152—but take care not to red line the engine. Normal climb power settings are more appropriate in higher-performance airplanes like a Mooney or Lance. Learn to set your power by feel and sound, with only a quick glance at the instruments to confirm your judgment. A prolonged look at the panel will cause you to let the plane's attitude go astray; precise attitude control in this maneuver demands virtually constant vigilance of outside references.

During the maneuver the plane can slip off your desired altitude for three reasons:

1. Incorrect pitch
2. Inappropriate power
3. Inconsistent bank

When you find your altitude error approaching either edge of your 100-foot tolerance, rapidly check each of these factors. First, check your pitch attitude against the outside horizon. Obviously, a nose held too high will cause the plane to climb, while a nose held too low will cause it to descend. If the nose is too high, you can lower it with no problem. But if the nose is too low, you must shallow the bank slightly as you lift the nose to its proper attitude. This will prevent the bank from over-steepening as you apply additional back pressure.

A higher-than-needed power setting will cause the plane to climb, even while you are holding proper pitch and roll. A power setting that is too low will, on the other hand, result in loss of altitude.

An inconsistent bank will, of course, cause the altitude to vary. If you allow the bank to shallow, the plane will climb. If the bank over-steepens, you will lose altitude—and you could suddenly find yourself in a spiral.

Verify your angle of bank by quick scans of the attitude indicator. There are common mistakes to keep in mind when interpreting this instrument during steep turns. Often a pilot disoriented in the maneuver will interpret the instrument *in reverse*. He will find himself steepening the bank when it should be shallowed. This occurs because the horizon line on the instrument face does the banking, rather than the wing symbol. Also, a confused pilot will often mistake the instrument's 90-degree index for the 60-degree mark. This error usually leads to a power spiral.

A spiral recovery presents no problem to a pilot, once he knows what to expect. A spiral is not a spin. It is merely a descent in a tight turn. But the sound and feel of a spiral can be disconcerting if you are caught unaware. Practice recovery from an intentional spiral and if you fall into one by accident, it will hold no surprises.

To set up the spiral, roll into a fairly steep turn and

let your nose down a bit . . . the spiral will develop. Listen as the rapidly increasing airspeed changes the engine's tone from a growl to a whine . . . the slipstream sounds like a firehose against your windscreen . . . and the controls stiffen to banjo-string firmness. Then level your wings, reduce your power, and watch as every-thing quickly returns to normal. The recovery is as simple as that.

Learn to cross-check pitch, roll, and power quickly and frequently. With practice, you will be able to check all three and make any necessary corrections in as many seconds. Keep your pitch attitude under constant surveillance; roll and power will need verifying at each 90-degree point of the maneuver, preferably as each reference line sweeps by below.

Small excursions in altitude (30 feet or less) can be easily corrected by slightly changing the bank. Steep-ening the bank a scant 3 or 4 degrees will lower the plane at a slow, steady rate. Similarly, the airplane may be raised by shallowing the bank a few degrees. If a large error in altitude should occur (in excess of 100 feet) you will save time by stopping the turn, returning to straight and level flight, and starting the maneuver over again.

The high power setting and nose-high attitude will cause torque forces to behave as though you were in a climb. Rudder must offset this torque action and must change as you change the direction of the turn. You will need to carry some right rudder throughout the right turn. At the crossover point of the maneuver, more rudder pressure will be needed when rolling from a left turn than from a right turn. Similarly, if the maneuver is ended from a left turn, more rudder will be required for the recovery.

Keep ahead of pitch control during the crossover in alternating the left and right turns. Slowly and steadily ease back pressure on the stick from its nose-high position in the turn to straight and level as the wings pass through their zero bank position. Then reapply back pressure as you bank into the opposite turn. Not hard to do—if you know where to hold your nose against the horizon during the turn.

Coordinate power with pitch during the crossover: ease the throttle back from high power to cruise as the wings pass through their level position. Then feed in the RPM's once more as you approach your 50-degree bank in the opposite direction.

On recovery, lower the nose to its level cruise attitude as you reduce throttle to cruise power.

The steep 720 turn, learned to perfection: the ability to fly skillfully under high G's and in an unusual attitude . . . against that day, low and slow over the numbers, you discover a plane lifting off from the opposite end of *your* runway . . . and closing fast.

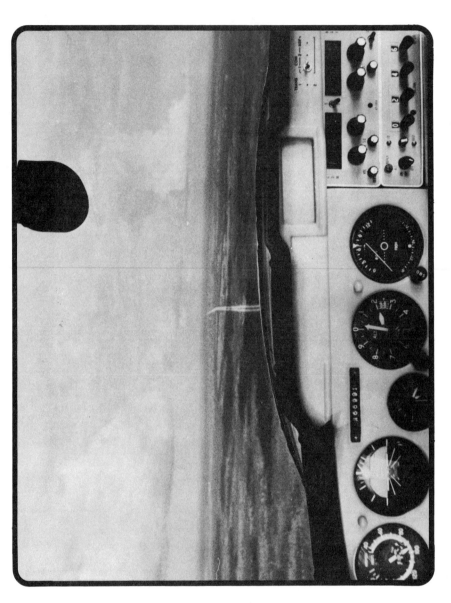

1 Line up on a straight road and enter your steep turn from straight and level flight.

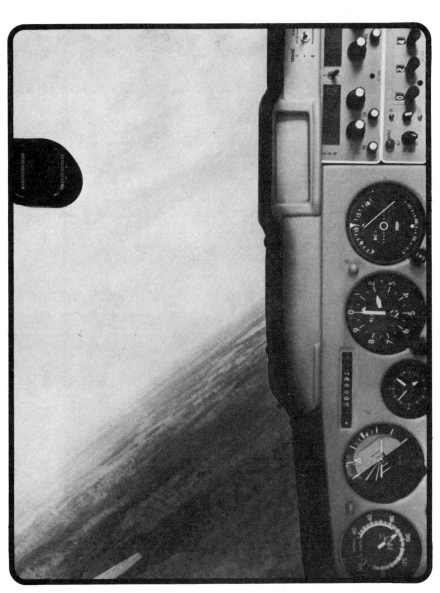

2 Roll into your first turn and reach a 50-degree bank within the initial 45 degrees of turn. Add power as you reach the steep bank and increase back pressure to prevent a loss of altitude. Complete two turns.

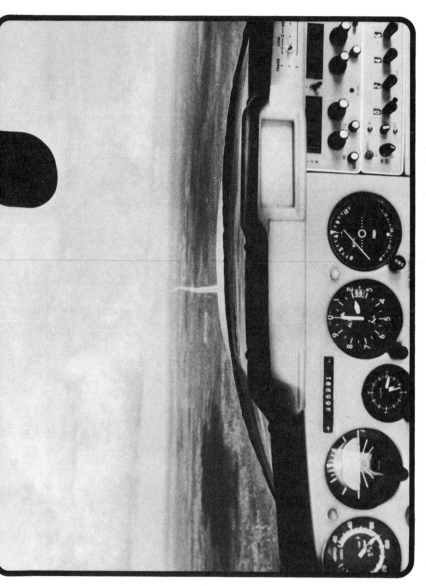

3 Relieve back pressure and decrease to cruise power during the crossover to the second turn—so that the plane's nose is level as it passes through your entry heading.

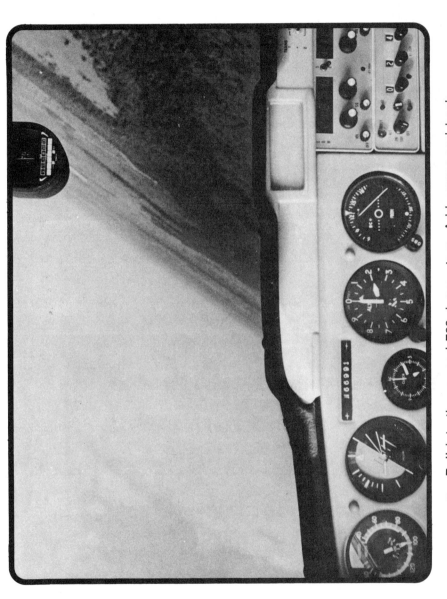

4 Roll into the second 720-degree turn. Add power and back pressure and haul the nose twice around again.

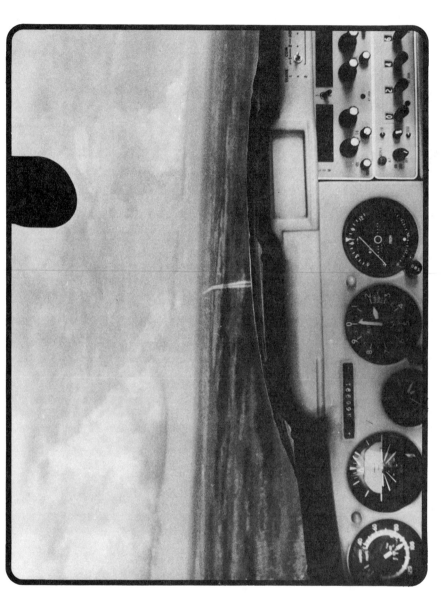

5 Complete the maneuver on your entry heading. Reduce power to cruise and level the nose as your wings roll into straight and level.

PRACTICE GUIDE—STEEP 720-DEGREE TURNS

Preflight Review

The Maneuver
Alternating left and right 720-degree turns at a 50-degree angle of bank.

Pilot Skills Developed
Precision control under high load factors. Orientation in extreme attitudes.

Performance Standards
Altitude: ± 100 feet
Bank: 50 degrees, ± 5 degrees.
Recovery heading: ± 10 degrees.
Controls: Coordinated throughout.

Performance Tips
* Use ground reference lines to maintain geographic and sensory orientation.
* The nose *appears* higher in the left turn than in the right turn, when flying from the left seat. *Know* your outside reference for a level nose in each direction of turn.
* Add power appropriate to your plane as bank nears 50 degrees. Full power in low-powered trainers. Normal climb power in higher-performance planes. Don't exceed engine red line.
* Maintain altitude by cross-checking for correct pitch attitude, power, bank.
* Correct small altitude-errors with slight variations in bank. Steepen bank to descend a few feet; shallow to climb.

* Torque forces act like left rudder while carrying high power and back pressure. Plane tends to slip or skid during crossover. Rolling from left to right requires more rudder than rolling from right to left.

Common Mistakes
* Losing track of your position within the turns. (Call out each 90 degrees as indicated by your ground references.)
* Lack of aggressiveness in quickly establishing the steep bank. (Cures itself with practice.)
* Leaning away from the steep turn. (Sit straight and hard against the back of the seat.)
* Failure to maintain a constant scan of outside visual references. (Learn to scan the panel with only a flick of the eyes.)
* Mistaking the attitude indicator's 90-degree index for the 60-degree mark. (Learn to recognize 50 degrees by the slant of the outside horizon.)

In-flight Practice Guide

Pre-entry
* Minimum entry altitude: 3000 AGL.
* Clear for other traffic.
* Turn on landing light/strobes.
* Align with ground reference lines.

Flying Steep 720-Degree Turns

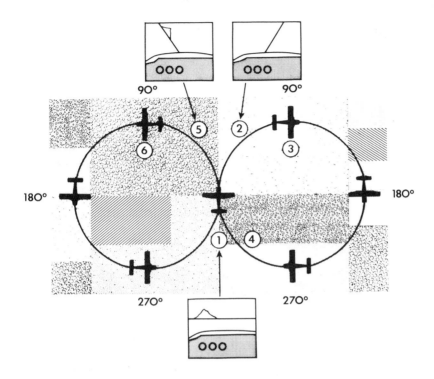

Keypoint 1. * Enter from straight and level at entry power (cruise or maneuvering, which- ever is slower).

* Roll into right turn.

Keypoint 2. * Establish 50 degrees of bank within 45 degrees of turn.

* Add appropriate power as bank nears 50 degrees (———RPM ———MP).

* Apply back pressure as wings reach 50- degree bank.

Keypoint 3. * Cross-check angle of bank and control coordination at each 90 degrees of right turn.

Keypoint 4. * Maintain the 50-degree bank until you are within 45 degrees of completing the right 720-degree turn.

Keypoint 5. * Reduce bank, power, back pressure as you reach crossover point.
* Roll into left turn.
* Establish 50 degrees of bank within 45 degrees of turn.
* Add appropriate power as bank nears 50 degrees.
* Apply back pressure as wings reach 50-degree bank.

Keypoint 6. * Cross-check angle of bank at each 90 degrees of turn.
* Recover to straight and level cruise during final 45 degrees of left 720-degree turn.

Notes for Review

THE
CHANDELLE

The chandelle is the logical maneuver to follow steep 720-degree turns. It uses the skills learned in the steep turns and further polishes them in preparation for the maneuvers to follow. The chandelle presents the same control coordination demands—keeping the ball centered while you turn with high power settings—but adds another factor: rapidly changing airspeed during the turn.

This maneuver also tests your ability to remain oriented and aware of the plane's attitude. But the elements that lead to disorientation are different from those in the steep turn. While high load factors are

missing in the chandelle, your ability to remain oriented is hampered by the plane's nose hiding your
view of the horizon during much of the maneuver. And
while the attitude of the chandelle is not as extreme as
the 50-degree banked steep turn, the chandelle asks
you to keep track of your position while you climb in
an oblique 180-degree turn, where visual clues can be
confusing.

Stated in its simplest terms, the chandelle is a maximum performance 180-degree climbing turn with
maximum altitude gain consistent with your selected
pitch and power (Figure 6). As a training exercise, however, the maneuver is more complex. A chandelle
properly flown requires eight specific and essential
steps (Figure 7):

1. Apply roll, pitch, and power in one-two-three sequence.
2. Establish and maintain your turn at an exact, predetermined angle of bank until reaching the 90-degree keypoint.
3. Establish climb attitude that, held constant, will produce
   the best-angle-of-climb speed at the top (180-degree
   point) of the maneuver.
4. Reach climb power prior to the 90-degree point of the
   turn.
5. Start your roll-out from the climbing turn at the exact
   90-degree point of the turn, *while* maintaining the correct climb attitude.
6. Set up a constant rate of roll-out that will result in the
   wings leveling at the 180-degree point of the maneuver.
7. Maintain coordinated controls throughout the maneuver.
8. Recover from your chandelle with a smoothly executed
   level-off that loses neither altitude nor reciprocal heading
   and keeps the ball centered.

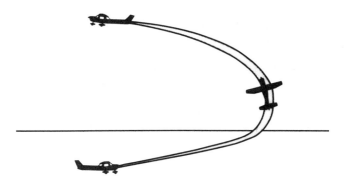

Figure 6
Stated in its simplest terms, the chandelle is a maximum 180-degree performance climbing turn with maximum altitude gain.

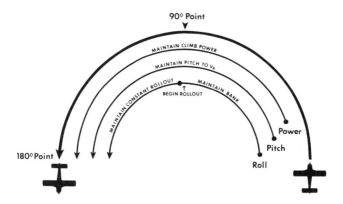

Figure 7
Roll, pitch, and power in the chandelle:
1. Apply roll, pitch, and power in one-two-three sequence.
2. Maintain a medium bank to the 90-degree point of the maneuver.
3. Maintain the pitch attitude that produces the best-angle-of-climb speed at the 180-degree point of the maneuver.
4. Advance the throttle to climb power.
5. Begin a smooth roll-out at the 90-degree point of the maneuver.
6. Recover to straight and level at the 180-degree point of the maneuver.

To call your maneuver a chandelle, it must exhibit each of these eight skills. If it doesn't, give the climbing turn another label—it is not a chandelle.

The chandelle was developed originally by French pilots flying their canvas-armored Nieuports over the trenches of World War I. They needed a fast, climbing 180 that would quickly bank them away from a Fokker's stream of tracers and grab the critical altitude advantage. The flight path of an expertly flown chandelle made their small biplanes a tough target to hit, and a young pilot's skill was often tested in a heartbeat's time.

Today, the chandelle is useful in developing a sense of timing, control coordination throughout a wide range of airspeeds, and an acute awareness of aircraft attitude. Good timing is essential here. You must, for example, roll decisively to the bank you desire, so that there is time to establish your climb attitude and power setting *prior* to reaching the turn's 90-degree point. And you must time your rate of roll-out from the 90-degree point so that the wings level just as you reach the 180-degree point. Your level-off has to be planned to regain cruise speed just as you lower the plane's nose to cruise attitude.

Control coordination is of the essence: Here you fly a fast, abrupt, climbing turn while the airspeed diminishes from cruise to a few knots above stall. Additionally, you perform the maneuver as both left and right turns, and each direction presents its own coordination challenges. Finally, you recover from a speed near minimum controllable airspeed and accelerate to cruise speed, all while keeping the ball centered against a slip or a skid.

To set up for the chandelle, align your plane with a north-south or east-west reference line, or any long, straight road. Enter above 2000 AGL from straight and level, at the lower of cruise or maneuvering speed. Apply roll, pitch, and power in one-two-three sequence. If you do so out of sequence or simultaneously, say to yourself *"roll-pitch-power."* This should do it— and also make you aware of the one-two-three sequence essential to a precision entry.

As you enter the chandelle, roll the wings quickly to the angle of bank that produces the maximum altitude gain in the maneuver. Bank too steeply and you will reach the 180-degree point before the engine and the plane's momentum has had a chance to pull you up to maximum altitude. If your bank is too shallow, the plane will slow to the region of reverse command before you reach the top of the maneuver. In modern low-performance planes, use a 30- to 35-degree bank; a bank of 20 to 25 degrees is appropriate for higher performance planes. Generally, the more horsepower available, the shallower the optimum bank, because planes with a larger reserve of power can continue to gain altitude over a longer period of time.

Once you establish the desired bank, hold it while you lift the plane's nose to its best-angle-of-climb pitch attitude. A number of pilots inadvertently let their bank steepen as they apply back pressure, unaware that they must apply slight opposite aileron and rudder as they increase pitch pressure in the turn. Back pressure in a turn, without compensating aileron and rudder, steepens the bank. Try a simple experiment to see this over-banking tendency develop: Roll into a medium-banked turn, then apply back pressure but *do not* move the ailerons or rudder, and watch the bank steepen.

The pitch attitude to set up is one that, when held constant, produces the plane's best-angle-of-climb speed just as you reach the 180-degree top of the maneuver. You may find it difficult to recognize this attitude because it is unfamiliar. It's doubly difficult to see, because you must gauge it while the airplane climbs in an oblique flight path. A simple drill will help you visually determine the reference for best-angle-of-climb speed: Put the plane in a climbing spiral and note the pitch attitude that maintains the best-angle airspeed as given in your manual.

Establish your roll and pitch just before you reach the 45-degree point of the chandelle to allow yourself time to bring in climb power before reaching the 90-degree point. If you're flying behind a small engine with a fixed prop, go ahead and mash in full power. The engine will not red line, because you have already lifted the nose to a high pitch attitude. If you fly a plane with a high-performance engine and a controllable propeller, however, excessive manifold pressure is possible. Advance the power only to its normal climb setting.

Begin to roll out of the turn at the exact 90-degree point of the maneuver. It takes a surprising amount of right rudder to start a roll-out from a left chandelle. (Very little left rudder is needed to roll from a *right* chandelle, however.) This is due to the torque forces at work. A quick look at the needle and ball tells whether or not you are using the correct rudder pressure. (If you have trouble coordinating your controls during the roll-out, practice alternating left and right turns while in a prolonged steep climb.)

Some pilots start the roll-out too late simply because they do not keep track of their position; they forget to keep tabs on their ground reference lines. Their eyes are aimed out over the upraised nose and, of course, see nothing but empty sky. *Meaningful* visual references will be found out the side window, toward the ground. Keep a close watch on the wing tip and its position relative to your ground reference lines and you can continually plot your plane's position in the flight path. Additionally, you can hold your desired nose-up pitch by observing the slant of your wing tip against the ground. This wing tip reference also helps to establish the proper, steady rate of roll-out.

The rate of roll-out begun at the 90-degree point must remain constant. Again, the correct rate will result in the wings leveling just as you reach the 180-degree point of the maneuver. Let's say you initially banked 30 degrees. In this case your roll-out must diminish your bank at the rate of 1 degree of bank for each 3 degrees of turn during the final 90 degrees of

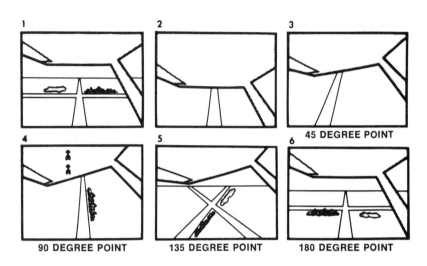

Figure 8

Once you start leveling your wings at the 90-degree point, gauge the upward movement of your wing tip to maintain a proper rate of roll-out.

1. Align your plane with a road, prior to maneuver entry, in order to easily recognize the 45- , 90- , 135- , and 180-degree points of the chandelle.
2. Enter maneuver by applying roll, pitch, and power in that sequence.
3. Establish roll, pitch, and power prior to the 45-degree point of the maneuver.
4. Begin a roll-out at the 90-degree point. Follow the upward progress of your wing tip.
5. At the 135-degree point, you are halfway through the recovery—and your bank should be half its original magnitude. Try to time the roll-out so that the wings level just as the plane reaches the 180-degree point.
6. Recover to straight and level flight at the 180-degree point.

the maneuver. Of course, that sort of arithmetic is a little hard to manage in the air; it's far better to determine the proper rate of roll visually: Just keep track of your wing tip's upward path against the ground (Figure 8). First, keep in mind how your wing tip appears relative to the horizon when the wings are level. Then simply follow the progress of your wing tip upward against the ground toward this level-wing position. As you follow the upward path of the wing tip, also track the plane's alignment with the 180-degree point of the turn. With a little practice you can make the two come out together.

Also use this wing-tip reference to grade the smoothness of your roll-out. If the wing tip stops momentarily before the wings are level, your rate of roll is not constant. If your wing-tip movement accelerates against the ground, you again know the roll is not constant.

Begin to lower the nose to its level cruise attitude the instant the wings roll level at the 180-degree (reciprocal) recovery heading. Many pilots let their chandelle go astray during the level-off process, simply because they feel that the maneuver is finished once the wings level from the turn. Such is not the case; the level-off is a definite phase of the maneuver.

As you level off, lower the nose to its level position very slowly. Because of the unusually slow climb speed, the airplane needs more time to accelerate to cruise. If you lower the nose at a normal level-off rate, a loss of altitude is certain. Of course, as in any level-off, keep the power at its climb setting until you regain cruise airspeed. Meanwhile, start to reduce right rudder pressure smoothly. Keep in mind that you began to level off from an unusually high pitch attitude, extremely low airspeed, and climb power. A heavy right foot was needed to keep the ball centered and the prop from biting into the wind sideways with a loud *"Brraap!"* (A skid makes the prop sound just like a carpenter's power saw biting sidewise into the wood . . . and for the same reason.) Rudder pressure must start to diminish the moment you begin to lower the nose and pick up airspeed. Continue to reduce rudder pressure until cruise speed is reestablished and the throttle is returned to cruise power as you complete the maneuver.

If you perform each of the eight essential steps of the maneuver with precision, you have flown the chandelle successfully. You have done some skillfully coordinated flying. And for an afternoon you have shared the heritage of those sputtering canvas and wooden biplanes of 1917.

1 Before you start your chandelle, line up on a road. It will help you identify the 45-, 90-, 135-, and 180-degree keypoints of the maneuver.

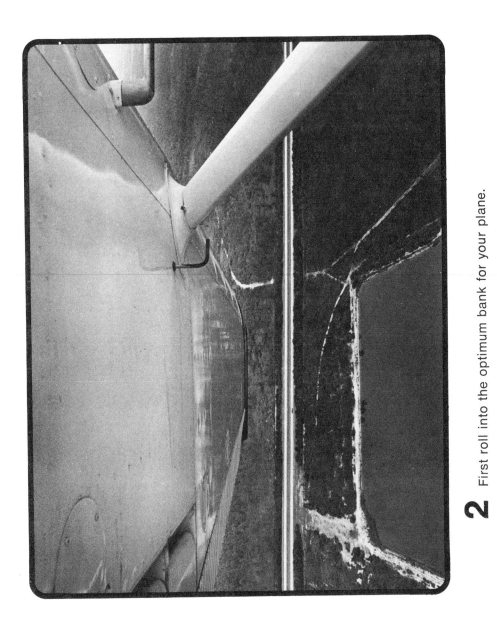

2 First roll into the optimum bank for your plane.

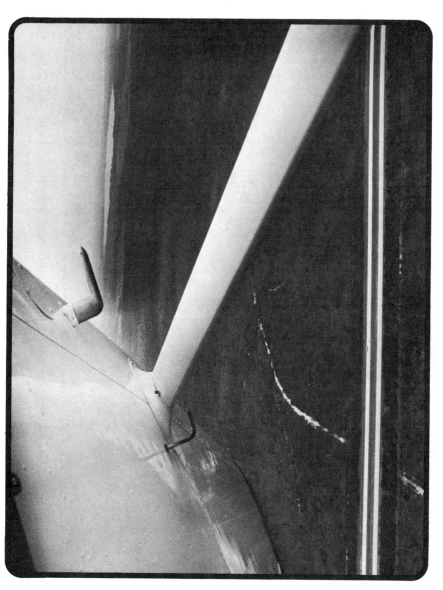

3 Then bring the nose up into a climb toward best-angle-of-climb speed and add power. Accomplish all this before the 45-degree keypoint.

4 At the 90-degree keypoint, begin a steady rate of roll-out that will level the wings at the 180-degree keypoint. Keep that nose climbing toward best-angle-of-climb speed.

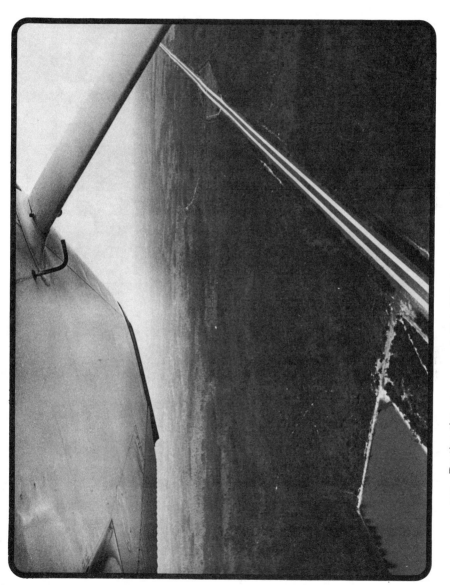

5 By the time you reach the 135-degree keypoint, your bank is only half its original steepness. But the nose is still climbing.

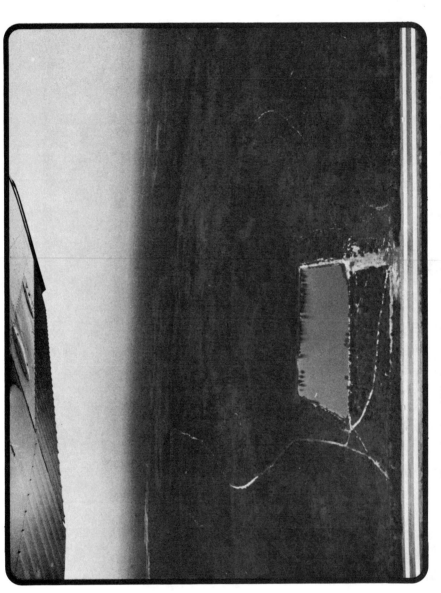

6 Reach the 180-degree keypoint just as the wings level and the upturned nose hits the best-angle-of-climb speed.

7 Slowly level the nose. Reduce to cruise power as you accelerate to cruise speed to complete the chandelle.

PRACTICE GUIDE—THE CHANDELLE

Preflight Review

The Maneuver

A 180-degree climbing turn with maximum altitude gain.

Pilot Skills Developed

Timing, control coordination, attitude awareness.

Performance Standards

Bank: $\pm$ 5 degrees.

Recovery heading: $\pm$ 10 degrees from reciprocal of entry heading.

Airspeed: $\pm$ 5 knots (5.7 MPH) of best-angle speed at the 180-degree keypoint.

Controls: Coordinated throughout.

Performance Tips

* Use ground reference lines to keep track of your progress through the maneuver.
* Use the lower of cruise speed or maneuvering speed as your entry airspeed.
* Use an angle of bank appropriate to your airplane. Low performance planes, 30- to 35-degree bank; higher performance planes, 20- to 25-degree bank.
* Know the pitch attitude that will result in best-angle-of-climb speed.
* Required rudder pressures will differ in each direction of turn: more to right, less to left.
* Use a climb power setting appropriate to your airplane. Full throttle in low-powered planes;

normal climb power in higher performance planes.

Common Mistakes

* Applying roll, pitch, and power simultaneously. (Say "roll-pitch-power" to yourself as you perform each function.)

* Allowing the desired bank to steepen as pitch increases. (Apply slight opposite aileron and rudder as you increase back pressure.)

* Losing track of your position within the climbing turn. (Look out the side window rather than through the windshield.)

* Delaying the roll-out past the 90-degree keypoint of the left climbing turn. (A *lot* of right rudder is needed to initiate the roll-out from the *left* chandelle.)

* Allowing an irregular rate of roll-out from the 90-degree point. (Watch your wing tip for a smooth upward movement.)

* Using an incorrect rate of roll-out that allows the wings to level either before or after the 180-degree keypoint of the maneuver. (Watch your plane's fuselage align with your straight road. Time your rate of roll so that the wing tip reaches zero bank just as the plane aligns with your 180-degree ground reference line.)

* Allowing the maneuver to deteriorate as recovery is made to straight and level cruise flight. (Lower the nose *slowly* to level. Reduce power *slowly* to cruise as the nose levels. Reduce rudder pressure *slowly* as the airspeed increases to cruise speed.)

In-flight Practice Guide

Pre-entry
  * Minimum entry altitude: 2000 AGL.
  * Clear for other traffic.
  * Turn on landing light/strobes.
  * Align with ground reference line.

Flying the Chandelle

Keypoint 1. * Enter from straight and level.
  * Entry airspeed: ——knots (——— MPH).
  * Roll to desired bank: ——degrees.

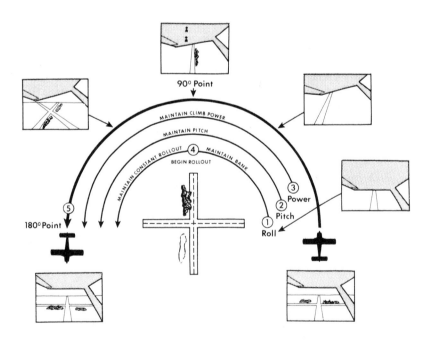

Keypoint 2. * Apply back pressure to best-angle-of-climb speed attitude.

Keypoint 3. * Apply power: ———RPM ———MP.

Keypoint 4. * Start roll-out at constant rate.

Keypoint 5. * Best-angle-of-climb speed: ———knots (———MPH).

* Slowly level nose as wings reach zero bank.

* Reduce to cruise power as plane accelerates to cruise speed.

Notes for Review

THE STEEP SPIRAL

While the chandelle is described as a maximum performance *climbing* turn, the *1080-degree steep spiral* is a precision *descending* turn. In this maneuver you glide your plane through a continuous turn of 1080 degrees (three times around) at a 50-degree bank, minimum power, and a descent speed 50 percent greater than your aircraft's V_{S1} stalling speed.

Learn to fly the steep spiral as two different maneuvers, each of which develops a different pilot skill. First, perform the maneuver as a *constant-bank* spiral, holding the 50-degree bank throughout the full three turns. Second, fly the maneuver as a *constant-radius* spiral, gliding downward about a point on the ground, varying your bank to compensate for the wind. With either maneuver, strive for a recovery heading within 10 degrees of entry heading. Don't let your airspeed stray more than 10 knots, and keep the controls coordinated throughout the spiral. Allow yourself a bank tolerance of only 5 degrees either side of 50. In the *constant-bank* spiral, try to stay within the 5-degrees tolerance *throughout* the descent. In the *constant-radius* spiral, this applies at the points of steepest bank.

The steep spiral develops a degree of immunity to disorientation and improves awareness of wind effects and airspeed control. Pilots new to the spiral sometimes become disoriented during the second or third turn. (You may want to practice your first few spirals with a 40-degree bank.) However, keeping track of your position by reference to landmarks minimizes disorientation.

Airspeed control is a challenge in the *constant-radius* spiral because you must vary your bank to compensate for the wind. And for a constant airspeed, you must vary elevator pressure as you change your bank. Not only are you required to maintain an exact airspeed while correcting for the wind, but the wind changes direction and velocity as you descend. (At 2000 AGL the wind will normally double its ground velocity and shift its direction 45 degrees to the right.)

After clearing the area for traffic, fly into entry position by aligning your plane with a north-south or east-west reference line. The ground reference lines minimize disorientation and verify your position at each 90 degrees of turn. By keeping count of the lines three times around, you will know when you have completed the full 1080 degrees. Also use the lines to ensure a recovery heading identical to your entry heading. There is little time to consult your heading indicator during the spiral.

Enter your spiral at an altitude that allows a *recovery* at least 1500 AGL when you have completed the three turns. You will want to determine, by trial, how many feet your plane loses in each 360 degrees of turn (about 500 feet for most planes).

Set up your airspeed and power setting *before* you roll into the spiral. Idle throttle works fine with the smaller engines. But if you are flying a higher performance aircraft, carry a touch of power to prevent rapid cooling of your engine. (The power setting you use on a short final works fine.) If this small amount of power makes your airplane pick up excess speed, fly the maneuver either with partial flaps or with gear down.

Practice your first few spirals with a maximum bank of 40 degrees. This slows the action a bit and gives you a chance to observe how the wind affects your ground track.

Once you feel at home with the bank/ground speed relationship, can visualize your ground track and crab angle, anticipate the changing control pressures—go ahead and steepen your spiral to the 50-degree mark. Just remember, anytime you feel disoriented or find the airspeed increasing, merely level your wings and watch everything return to normal.

Constant-Bank Spiral Once you establish your entry airspeed (1.5 × stall [V_{S_1}]), roll to a 50-degree bank. The attitude indicator is useful in establishing your bank in the first few spirals—but learn to recognize your angle of bank by referring to the outside horizon.

Use the natural horizon for the pitch attitude that produces the correct airspeed. This outside reference differs between left and right turns if you fly a side-by-side airplane, as in any steep turn. Remember, a small pitch change produces a considerable airspeed change. And don't chase your airspeed needle as you search for the proper pitch attitude. Instead, make a small pitch change and pause to see what change in airspeed develops. The attitude indicator also helps set up a proper pitch attitude—if you are aware that a pitch change of one-half dot on the attitude indicator equals 5 knots in nearly all modern light airplanes.

Airspeed in the spiral varies for one of two reasons. It wanders if you don't maintain a constant bank or if you let your pitch go astray. Usually the fault in a constant-bank spiral is inconsistent bank. If the bank shallows, the airspeed dissipates; if the bank steepens, the airspeed increases. The attitude indicator tells you. Correct the bank to correct the airspeed.

Begin recovery when your plane is within 45 degrees of your entry heading. A rapid, coordinated roll-out, as you reduce back pressure and restore cruise power, concludes your *constant-bank* steep spiral.

Constant-Radius Spiral　　When you feel comfortable flying the steep spiral with a constant bank, add some complexity to the maneuver. Add a factor that helps develop a feel for airspeed control—add the effects of wind. Rather than hold a *constant* bank, *vary* your bank as necessary to compensate for the wind as you descend in a *constant-radius* spiral around a reference point on the ground. Here you maintain precise descent airspeed while constantly changing your angle of bank. Of course, the changing bank also changes load, drag, and lift factors; these complicate your airspeed control. The airspeed tends to increase with a steep bank and to decrease as you shallow your bank. Control of the airplane is made even more complex because much of your attention is directed outside the plane, as you eyeball your ground reference point to gauge any drift.

Let's see how best to handle the two distinct parts of the steep constant-radius 1080-degree spiral: maintaining a constant-radius ground track *and* a constant airspeed during descent.

For a constant-radius ground track, compensate for *changing ground speed* (as your head-wind or tail-wind component changes) and for *wind drift.* These are two distinct and separate corrections.

While you descend around your ground reference point, vary your *rate of turn* as your *ground speed* varies in order to stay on the desired ground track. A faster ground speed requires a faster rate of turn; a slower ground speed requires a slower rate of turn, if the radius of turn is to remain constant.

This relationship between speed and rate of turn affects a turning automobile in the same manner. Picture yourself driving a car at 30 MPH. Ahead lies a curve about a quarter-mile long that changes your course by about 60 degrees. At your slow speed of 30 MPH, you are in that turn about thirty seconds. You have to turn your car at a rate of turn of 2 degrees per second—so you turn your steering wheel slowly.

Now—put yourself behind the wheel of that same car but approaching the curve at 60 MPH. At the faster speed you are in that curve only fifteen seconds. You need a faster (degrees per second) rate of turn, and you turn the steering wheel harder to get it. Of course, you do not calculate the rate of turn as you drive through the curve. You just use your sense of timing—along with the visual reference provided by the centerline.

In an airplane a turn that follows a desired ground track is governed by the same relationship between ground speed and required rate of turn. But there are differences between turning a car and turning an airplane. In a plane our ground speed changes constantly throughout the turn as our head-wind or tail-wind component changes. And in a plane we control our rate of turn with angle of bank: the steeper the bank, the greater the rate of turn.

Follow through with the pilot in Figure 9 as he de-

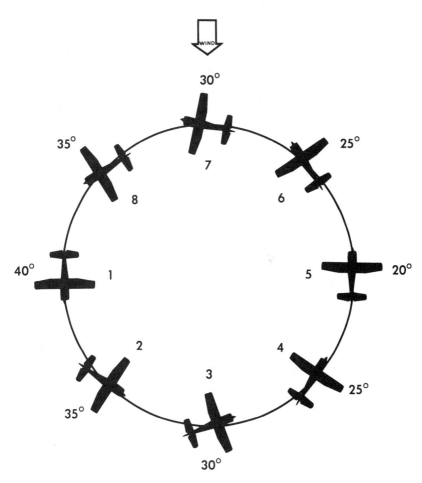

Figure 9
Your bank must shallow or steepen to match changes in ground speed.

1. Direct tail wind=highest ground speed=steepest bank.
2. Quartering tail wind=lower ground speed=shallower bank.
3. No tail wind=lower ground speed=shallower bank.
4. Quartering head wind=lower ground speed=shallower bank.
5. Direct head wind=lowest ground speed=shallowest bank.
6. Quartering head wind=higher ground speed=steeper bank.
7. No head wind=higher ground speed=steeper bank.
8. Quartering tail wind=higher ground speed=steeper bank.

scends along the desired ground track of his constant-radius spiral. The pilot enters the spiral at Point 1 with a direct tail wind. Since the greatest ground speed is realized at this point, our pilot enters the maneuver using his maximum bank (40 degrees in our illustration). Immediately passing this point he begins to lose his tail wind (Points 2 and 3) and progressively shallows his bank in order to reduce his rate of turn to match his dissipating ground speed. The pilot continues to shallow his bank through Point 4 as he continues to lose ground speed. Bank and ground speed continue to lessen until the plane meets a direct head wind at Point 5. At this point (slowest ground speed) the plane is at its shallowest bank (20 degrees in our illustration).

As soon as the pilot passes through Point 5, the plane begins to lose its head-wind component. Ground speed begins to increase (Point 6), and so must the bank. At Point 7 the plane continues to gain ground speed as its position changes from a head wind to a tail wind. And the pilot continues to steepen his bank through Point 8, until he returns to the direct tail-wind position of Point 1 and again rolls to his steepest bank. (The steepest bank does *not* occur at Point 3. Something unique does occur at this point—as we shall soon see—but it has nothing to do with bank.)

Test your understanding of the relationship between ground speed and bank. Let's *reverse* the direction of the turn, shift the wind around 90 degrees, and *match* the pairs of *equal banks* in Figure 10. The correct answers are:

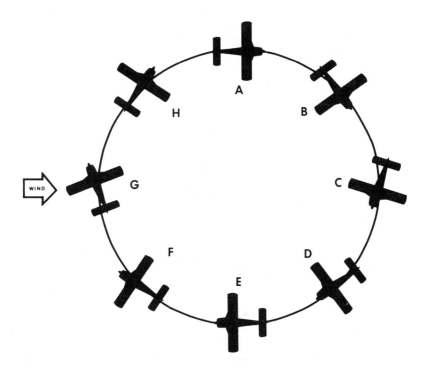

Figure 10
Test yourself: Match the pairs of planes requiring equal banks.

B = H (ground speeds are equal, each has a quartering tail wind)

C = G (ground speeds are equal, each has a direct
crosswind)

D = F (ground speeds are equal, each has a quartering head wind)

Pilots often find it difficult to match their bank to
their ground speed, for two reasons. First, they lose

track of the wind direction (and an unexpected change in ground speed catches them by surprise). Second, they don't visualize the desired ground track. (Remember how the centerline provided a visual reference that helped you steer the car through the turn?)

For both reasons a crossroads makes an excellent reference point to spiral down to. The intersection helps you keep tabs on the wind direction *at the surface.* (But remember that the wind shifts direction and increases in velocity at altitude. At 2000 to 3000 AGL, the wind usually shifts 45 degrees to the right of its surface direction, and it doubles in velocity. So as you spiral downward, anticipate a wind shift to the *left* and a *decrease* in velocity.)

A crossroads also helps you *visualize* your ground track (Figure 11). Just pick four landmarks, one along each arm of the intersection, equidistant from the center point. Then visualize a circle on the ground, connecting all four points. If your crossroads intersection lies in a developed area, property lines that appear as differently textured surfaces provide these waypoints around your center point. Telephone poles do the same job, so do an equal number of centerline stripes radiating from each branch of the intersection. How far from your center point should your landmarks lie? A constant-radius spiral with a maximum bank of 40 degrees needs a turning radius of about 1700 feet (about a third of a mile). A spiral with a 50-degree bank needs about a 1300-foot radius (a quarter of a mile).

In addition to compensating for wind-induced varia-

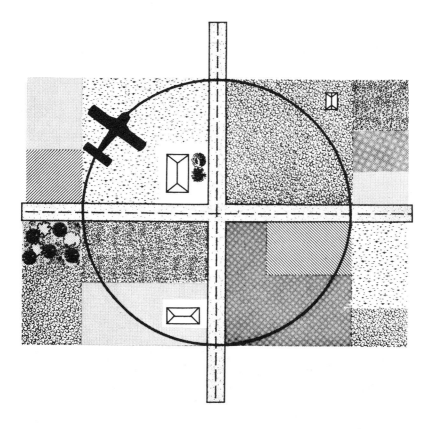

Figure 11
Choose a crossroads as your center point, to visualize easily your constant-radius ground track. Property lines often provide equidistant landmarks along each branch. So do an equal number of centerline stripes radiating from each branch.

tions in ground speed, also allow for wind drift. It is easy to visualize the crab angle required to fly a straight ground track (Figure 12). It is not so easy, however, to visualize the crab angle (wind correction angle) to fly a curved ground track (Figure 13). It is just as important, however, as it is during straight and level flight. If you do not crab as you descend through your spiral, you will lose your desired constant radius. Without wind-drift correction, your plane will fly an egg-shaped ground track. It will drift in too close on the upwind side of the center point and out too far on the downwind side. Your crab angle should vary constantly throughout your spiral, depending on how the crosswind component of the moment is affecting your desired ground track.

Use the four landmarks equidistant from the spiral's center to plan ahead for the necessary drift correction. When you see that you have a landmark "made" (even before you reach it), plan ahead to the next landmark, anticipating the wind in the next quarter-circle.

To maintain a constant-radius ground track, then, you must compensate for changing ground speed *and* wind drift.

For a constant descent airspeed in constant-radius spirals, keep in mind that incorrect pitch attitude is usually responsible for any airspeed error. The pilot fails to maintain a correct pitch as he varies his bank to correct for the wind. He tends to let the plane's nose rise as he shallows his bank, and to let the nose dip as he steepens his bank. Elevator pressure must vary as he varies his angle of bank.

Slightly vary back pressure throughout the spiral to hold a constant airspeed. Load factors, drag, and lift forces change all during the constant-radius spiral.

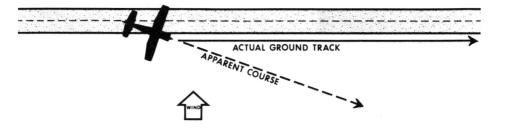

Figure 12
It is easy to visualize the wind correction needed when tracking along a road in straight and level flight.

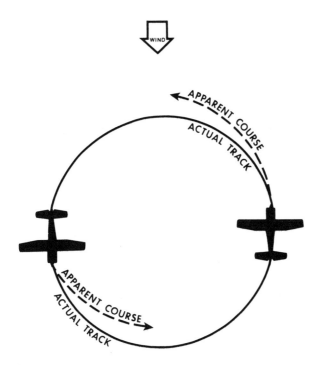

Figure 13
It is just as necessary to correct for drift during a turn, as it is during straight and level flight.

Load factors increase and lift forces decrease as you steepen your bank, and the plane's nose wants to dip. Conversely, when you shallow your bank into the wind, the load and lift forces reverse, and the plane's nose tends to rise. Compensate for these changing forces with elevator: Increase back pressure as you steepen the bank, and relieve it as you shallow the bank.

Again, let's follow through with the pilot spiraling downward in Figure 9. At Point 1 the plane is moving at its fastest ground speed. To compensate, the pilot applies his steepest bank at this point. This subjects his plane to the greatest load factor and least lift factor. To prevent the plane's nose from dipping (and picking up airspeed), he applies greater back pressure. Immediately after passing through Point 1 the pilot starts to shallow his bank—and starts to reduce back pressure. The bank continues to shallow through Points 2, 3, and 4, and back pressure is further reduced. At Point 5 the plane is in a direct head-wind position at its shallowest bank. Then he starts to increase both stick pressure and bank as the plane continues around through Points 6, 7, and 8 toward the direct tail-wind position of Point 1. Three times around with recovery to straight and level within 10 degrees of entry heading completes the maneuver successfully.

The constant-radius 1080 steep spiral presents the pilot with a twofold challenge: holding to a specific ground track at a specified airspeed.

Can the steep spiral—a circling descent at a precise airspeed over a desired ground point—find a useful role in your flying? Possibly—if and when you are faced with a forced landing and spot a field below. Useful? It could save the day!

PRACTICE GUIDE—THE STEEP SPIRAL

Preflight Review

The Maneuver

Drill 1: A spiral of three turns (1080 degrees) while maintaining a constant 50-degree bank and descent airspeed.

Drill 2: A spiral of three turns (1080 degrees) while maintaining a constant radius and descent airspeed.

Pilot Skills Developed

Drill 1: Resistance to disorientation.

Drill 2: Precise airspeed control. Awareness of wind effects.

Performance Standards

Airspeed: ± 10 knots (5.7 MPH).

Recovery heading: ± 10 degrees of entry heading.

Controls: Coordinated throughout.

Bank: Within 5 degrees (Drill 1).

Ground track: Constant radius (Drill 2).

Performance Tips

Drills 1 and 2:

* Determine by trial how many feet your plane descends in a 360-degree gliding turn.
* Set up the 1.5 × stall airspeed before entry.
* Practice first few spirals using a 40-degree maximum bank.
* Recover if you become disoriented or speed accelerates to cruise.

Drill 2 (Constant Radius):

* Use a road intersection for ground reference.
* 40-degree spiral (at steepest point) requires

1700-foot radius. 60-degree spiral requires 1300-foot radius.

* Visualize circle by choosing four landmarks along roads, equidistant from center point.
* Use crossroads intersection to count three times around and to determine recovery heading.
* Vary the angle of bank to compensate for variations in ground speed; the faster the ground speed, the greater the rate of turn required.
* Wind direction will shift left as you descend.

Common Mistakes

* Overcorrecting an errant airspeed. (Use small pitch changes, and allow them time to change the airspeed.)
* Failure to coordinate pitch control with variations in bank. (As you steepen the bank, increase back pressure to hold the airspeed in check. When you shallow the bank, decrease back pressure.)
* Losing track of the wind direction. (Visualize the wind crossing your road intersection.)
* Not planning for wind drift. (When you see you have a landmark "made," plan ahead to the next landmark, anticipating the wind in the next quarter-circle.)

In-flight Practice Guide

Pre-entry
* Minimum entry altitude: ——— AGL to allow 1500 AGL recovery.
* Clear for other traffic.
* Turn on landing light/strobes.
* Establish entry airspeed: ——— knots (——— MPH).

Flying the Steep Spiral

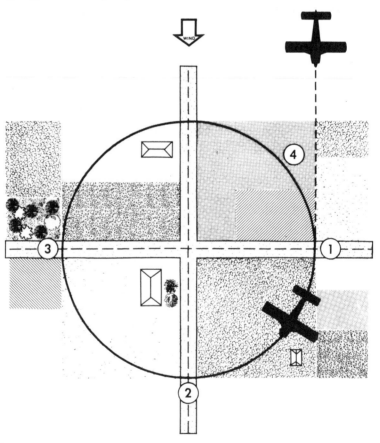

Drill 1:   Constant-Bank Spiral

Keypoint 1: * Roll to desired bank.

            * Apply back pressure to maintain entry airspeed.

Keypoint 2 * Verify your airspeed at each 90 degrees of turn. Make small adjustments to pitch if needed.

Keypoint 3 * Keep tabs on your ground reference lines at each 90 degrees of turn, to minimize disorientation.

Keypoint 4 * Begin recovery to level flight during final 45 degrees of your third turn.

            * Recover on entry heading.

Drill 2:   Constant-Radius Spiral

Keypoint 1 * Enter downwind over road intersection.

            * Roll to steepest desired bank and apply back pressure.

            * Bank must start to diminish as you lose direct tail wind.

Keypoint 2 * Bank continues to diminish as ground speed continues to diminish.

            * Back pressure lessens to maintain entry airspeed.

Keypoint 3 * Slowest ground speed requires least bank and back pressure.

            * Bank and back pressure must begin to increase as you leave this keypoint.

Keypoint 4 * Effect your recovery to level flight within 45 degrees of your third turn.

            * Recover on entry heading.

Notes for Review

LAZY EIGHTS

Flying is like a wiener roast. You have to share it to enjoy it. And there is no better way to share flying than to take a buddy aloft and show him the symmetrical beauty of a *lazy eight*—from the inside.

Viewed from above, the maneuver follows a ground track of two simple 180-degree S-turns (Figure 14). (The term "lazy eight" stems from this: If your spinner were a pencil point, the maneuver would trace out a figure eight against the horizon—an eight lying on its side.) But as Figure 15 shows, during the simple S-turn ground track you are *also* flying the plane through a

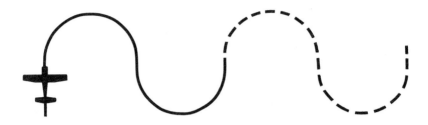

Figure 14
Viewed from above, the lazy eight follows a ground track of two simple 180-degree S-turns.

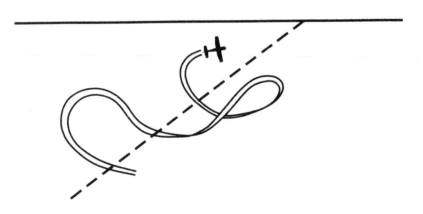

Figure 15
The Lazy eight is a pair of alternating precision 180-degree climbing and descending turns in opposite directions.

series of precision climbs and descents. A good lazy eight contains eleven essential qualities.

1. The airplane's pitch and roll change constantly throughout the maneuver.

2. Altitude at the top of each climb is the same at the 90-degree keypoint of each turn.
3. Altitude at the bottom of each descent is the same at the 180-degree keypoint of each turn.
4. Airspeed at the top of each climb is the same at the 90-degree point of each turn (best-angle-of-climb speed).
5. The airspeed at the base of each descent is the same at the 180-degree keypoint of each turn (cruise or maneuvering speed).
6. Maximum nose-up pitch and lowest nose-down pitch occur respectively at the 45-degree and 135-degree keypoints of each turn.
7. Maximum bank occurs at the 90-degree point of each turn (45-degree bank).
8. The nose cuts down through the horizon at the 90-degree point of each turn.
9. Each turn is an exact 180-degree change in direction.
10. The wings and nose each reach their level attitudes *simultaneously* as the plane reaches the 180-degree keypoints of each turn.
11. Controls coordinated throughout, ball centered.

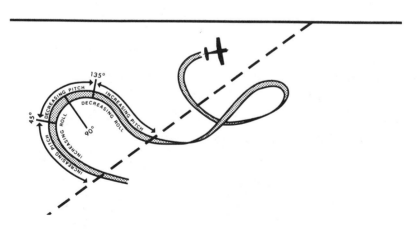

Figure 16

The lazy eight is the ultimate precision maneuver for developing and testing a pilot's planning ability, timing, and control coordination. The pilot *plans* the amount of power and pitch that produces the desired altitude and airspeed changes. He *times* his roll-out and level-off at the base of each turn so that the plane's nose and wings level simultaneously at the exact 180-degree points within the maneuver. And he keeps his controls *coordinated* throughout the turning climbs and descents that range in airspeed from cruise speed to best-angle-of-climb speed. Planning, timing, and coordination are made more complex because the pilot has to reverse his direction of elevator pressure while the direction of aileron and rudder pressures remain constant. All the skills developed in the steep turns, chandelles, and spirals is put into play as you fly a lazy eight.

You have to be able to recognize quickly the entry position and the 45-, 90-, 135-, and 180-degree keypoints of each turn as you fly the maneuver. To orient yourself, align the plane with north-south or east-west ground reference lines, or a prominent straight road, before starting the drill. Avoid practicing your lazy eights when the wind exceeds 15 knots. A light breeze will not drift your plane significantly during the course of the two 180-degree turns of a lazy eight. The drift of a strong wind, however, will carry you away from your ground reference and spoil the symmetry of your maneuver.

Enter the lazy eight at 2000 AGL minimum from straight and level cruise speed in low performance aircraft, maneuvering speed in high performance aircraft. Maintain this constant throttle setting throughout the maneuver. Start the maneuver by climbing into a turn —apply pitch and roll simultaneously (Figure 16). Plan your pitch pressure so that it can be steadily increased up to the 45-degree keypoint of the first climbing turn at a rate that will produce the plane's best-angle-of-climb speed by the time you reach the 90-degree keypoint in the turn. Also plan your pitch control so that the maximum altitude gained is the same at the top of each turn. Simultaneously roll the wings at a rate that will result in a 45-degree bank at the 90-degree keypoint.

Since pitch and roll change constantly (often one increasing in magnitude while the other decreases), let's follow pitch and roll separately throughout the initial climbing and descending turns. Pitch first: Steadily increase back pressure until maximum nose-up pitch is reached at the 45-degree keypoint (Figure 17). At this point, reverse elevator movement and gradually decrease back pressure. (The airspeed continues to

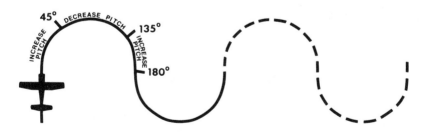

Figure 17
Nose-up pitch changes in the lazy eight.

dissipate for another moment, until you reach the approximate 90-degree keypoint.) Continue to decrease back pressure so that the plane's nose cuts down through the horizon at the 90-degree keypoint and the nose reaches its lowest pitch at the 135-degree keypoint of the descending turn. At the 135-degree keypoint, again reverse elevator and begin to lift the nose. Increase back pressure at a rate that levels the plane's nose at the 180-degree keypoint, aligned with the ground reference line.

Now for roll: Simultaneously vary your bank to produce a symmetrical turn (Figure 18). Start the turn as you lift your nose into the maneuver. Smoothly establish a rate of roll with gradually increasing aileron and rudder pressure for a 45-degree bank at the 90-degree keypoint of the first turn. Then, at this point, reverse aileron and rudder to begin a rate of roll-out that will level the wings at the 180-degree keypoint.

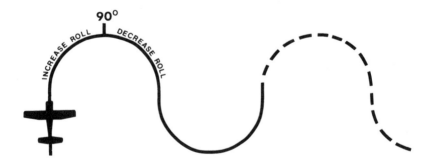

Figure 18
Roll variations in the lazy eight.

Let's review Figure 16 and follow the control movements through the initial climbing and descending turn:

1. Pitch and roll pressure both increase to the 45-degree keypoint.
2. Then elevator pressure decreases while roll continues to increase to the steepest bank at the 90-degree keypoint.
3. At this point, roll begins to decrease, while forward pressure continues to increase, for lowest nose-pitch at the 135-degree keypoint.
4. At the 135-degree point, stick pressure reverses again to lift the nose, while bank continues to decrease.
5. Nose-up pitch and decreasing roll are then timed to produce straight and level flight at the 180-degree keypoint.
6. Fly through the 180-degree point and up into the succeeding climbing and descending turn to complete the lazy eight.

Sounds complicated, doesn't it?

I once met a pilot who claimed he developed the required dexterity by learning to pat his head and rub his belly simultaneously, all the while whistling "The Stars and Stripes Forever" and mentally computing the square root of his plane's gross weight. I'm sure his system worked. There is, however, a more practical system of understanding and mastering the lazy eight. Let's break the maneuver down into its parts and see what problems usually arise within them:

1. *Pitch and roll applied simultaneously on entry.* Strangely enough, many pilots are unable to perform this task when they attempt their first few lazy eights. The carry-over from the chandelle's technique causes

them to apply pitch and roll separately. You can test your own performance by closely watching your plane's attitude against the horizon as you enter the maneuver. Chances are, you will notice one of two errors:

a. The nose starts to move upward toward the horizon *before* the wings start to bank, or
b. The wings start to bank *before* the nose starts to move upward.

To remedy this, practice a few climbing turns (maintaining cruise power) while consciously applying pitch and roll simultaneously.

2. *Constant rate of roll resulting in a 45-degree bank at the 90-degree point.* Difficulties in this segment usually stem from three sources, which combine to produce unfamiliar control responses.

First, the pitch-changes during the climbing turn affect the rate of roll you want to establish. Your bank tends to over-steepen as you apply back pressure during the first 45-degrees of the turn. Similarly, your bank tends to shallow as you apply forward pressure from the 45-degree point to the 135-degree point.

Second, the climbing turn involves changes in airspeed while at a constant (cruise) power setting. As you climb toward the 90-degree point, your airspeed varies from cruise speed to best-angle-of-climb speed. This, of course, imparts varying responsiveness to the aileron controls. This will help: Review aileron control at low speed by practicing climbing S-turns in slow-flight.

Third, your effort to maintain a rate of roll that produces a 45-degree bank at the top of the maneuver is complicated by changing torque forces. Because of torque effects you need considerable right rudder in the right climbing turns and very little rudder in the left climbing turns. This causes many pilots to over-bank at the top of the right turns.

3. *Constant rate of pitch change for approximately best-angle-of-climb speed at the top of the maneuver.* You don't have to deliver an *exact* predetermined air-speed at the 90-degree point of each climbing turn. But you must deliver the *same* airspeed at the top of each climbing turn—one close to the plane's best-angle-of-climb speed (within a five-knot—5.7 MPH—tolerance). You should also reach the same airspeed at the base of each diving turn, very near cruising speed.

It's not easy to deliver the same airspeed at the tops. Some flyers aren't sure what pitch attitude achieves a certain airspeed at the 90-degree point. Nor are they sure of the visual reference (against the horizon) that locates the correct pitch attitude for the desired air-speed. If you have difficulty here, establish best-angle-of-climb speed in a climbing spiral. This drill offers an unhurried look at the pitch attitude you will need at the 45-degree point of the maneuver. Be sure to prac-tice this with both left and right turns.

Compare airspeeds at the tops of your lazy eight turns to evaluate the quality of your pitch control. If the airspeeds are unequal at the 90-degree point of each climbing turn, then you did not apply the same pitch in both directions of the turns.

While the highest nose-up attitude occurs at the 45-

degree point of the turn, the slowest airspeed occurs at the 90-degree points. The plane's diminished momentum causes this. The maximum nose-down attitude occurs at the 135-degree point of the maneuver, but the plane's inertia keeps it from reaching its maximum speed until it reaches the 180-degree point.

4. *Constant power setting for equal altitudes at the tops and bases of the maneuver.* The basic lazy eight is flown with the same power setting throughout, and the one you choose has to produce climbing turns to the same maximum altitudes and descending turns to the same minimum altitudes. (A good lazy eight will climb about 500 feet.) Obviously a power setting that is too high causes the entire maneuver to gain altitude progressively with each set of turning climbs and descents. An insufficient power setting, on the other hand, causes the maneuver to lose altitude.

Before you try lazy eights, determine your plane's constant power setting by flying a series of gentle climbs and descents at cruise power, and keep it there. Level from your climbs at cruise speed. Then note whether your series of climbs and descents gained or lost altitude—make the power adjustment accordingly. Knowing the correct power setting beforehand tells you that any altitude inconsistencies are due to improper pitch control.

5. *Constantly changing pitch and roll control throughout the maneuver.* In lazy eights, you cannot allow pitch or roll to stabilize at any time. You are either raising or lowering the nose or rolling into or out

of a turn, or both. The elevator, ailerons, and rudder never stop moving. Problems with this invariably arise at the keypoints where a control pressure is reversed. Elevator pressure at the 45- and 135-degree points changes quickly from back to forward. Problems with roll also occur at these points.

Start forward pressure precisely at the 45-degree point. If you do not, the symmetry of your flight path suffers. First, the plane's nose will cut down through the horizon *beyond* the 90-degree point of the maneuver. (Conversely, premature forward pressure will cause the nose to cross the horizon *before* you reach the 90-degree point.) Second, the plane will reach the 180-degree point with a nose-high attitude rather than straight and level.

If you don't increase back pressure at the 135-degree point, the plane will exceed cruise speed as it hits the 180-degree point, and it is certain to descend below your desired altitude.

The reverse in direction of roll needed at the top of the maneuver also causes problems. If it is not done with exact timing—if you delay the roll-out—the plane's nose cuts down through the horizon well beyond the 90-degree point. Conversely, an early roll-out drops the nose down through the horizon too soon.

You can check for proper rate of roll by glancing at the attitude indicator as you fly through the 135-degree point. The angle of bank should have decreased to 20 or 25 degrees by that time. If you have not achieved this rate by then, you will probably reach the 180-degree position with the wings still banked.

The airplane's attitude at the 180-degree point of your turns testifies to your overall performance. You've got to fly skillfully all five segments of the lazy eight if the plane is to reach the 180-degree point within these tolerances:

1. Within 50 feet of entry altitude at each 180-degree point
2. Within five knots (5.7 MPH) of entry airspeed
3. Within 10 degrees of the entry heading
4. With wings level
5. With nose level
6. With controls coordinated

Follow this rule when practicing a series of lazy eights: Discontinue (and then reenter) the series any time the plane reaches the 180-degree position in an incorrect attitude. To continue the maneuver under these circumstances causes an incorrect entry to the next climbing turn, and the overall maneuver has no chance for success.

Learn to fly lazy eights to your very best ability. Then invite a friend aboard. Take him to altitude and show him flying at its very best—a lazy eight viewed from the cockpit.

1 Use a ground reference line for ease in determining the 40-, 90-, 135-, and 180-degree points of each loop of the lazy eight. Enter the maneuver by applying pitch and roll simultaneously.

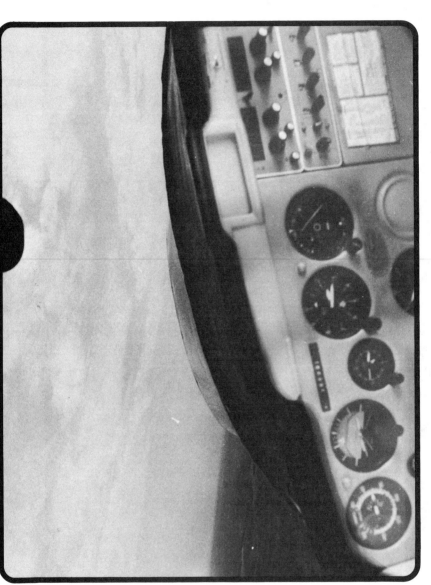

2 At the 45-degree point your roll is still increasing, but you begin relieving back pressure. Your angle of bank should be about half the amount you want at the 90-degree keypoint.

3 Airspeed is at its lowest as you near the 90-degree point. Begin reducing your bank but continue to relieve back pressure. The nose should slice down through the horizon at the 90-degree point.

4 At the 135-degree point your nose is at its lowest pitch, and your engine gains a few RPM's. Start lifting your plane's nose at this point and continue to roll out of your turn.

5 Arrive at the 180-degree keypoint with level nose and wings, at your entry altitude. Turn smoothly into the second loop of your lazy eight.

PRACTICE GUIDE—LAZY EIGHTS

Preflight Review

The Maneuver

A pair of alternating left and right climbing and descending 180-degree turns in opposite directions.

Pilot Skills Developed

Planning.

Timing.

Precise control coordination.

Performance Standards

At the 180-degree point of each turn:

Altitude: $\pm$ 50 feet of entry altitude.

Airspeed: $\pm$ 5 knots (5.7 MPH) of entry airspeed.

Heading: $\pm$ 10 degrees of entry heading.

Bank: Level.

Pitch: Level.

Controls: Coordinated.

Performance Tips

* Practice in either light wind or no wind to ensure symmetry of turns.
* Practice over a long, straight ground reference line to assist recognition of the 45-, 90-, 135-, and 180-degree keypoints.
* Pitch and roll are applied simultaneously on entry.
* Use a constant rate of roll that results in a 45-degree bank at the 90-degree point of each turn.
* You need considerable right rudder in the right

climbing turn and very little rudder in the left climbing turn—due to torque.

* Use a constant pitch change that results in best-angle-of-climb speed at the 90-degree points in the turns.
* Determine, by trial, the power setting that produces equal altitudes at the tops and bases of the maneuver.
* Keep the controls moving in a constant state of pitch and roll changes throughout the maneuver.

Common Mistakes

* Entering the maneuver by applying pitch and roll separately. (A holdover from the chandelle.)
* Producing inconsistent airspeeds at the 45-degree point of each climb. (Memorize the visual reference for the required pitch attitude.)
* Failure to keep the controls coordinated. (Allow for changing torque forces at varying airspeeds.)
* Failure to achieve desired bank at the 90-degree point. (Allow for changing aileron response at varying airspeeds.)
* Letting the nose fly down through the horizon before reaching the 90-degree point. (Probably released back pressure before reaching the 45-degree point.)
* Letting the nose fly down through the horizon after the 90-degree point has passed. (Probably released back pressure after passing the 45-degree point.)
* Failure to keep pitch and roll constantly chang-

ing. (Usually happens when a pilot is uncertain of his position within the maneuver.)

* Allowing excess speed to develop at the 180-degree point. (Apply more back pressure at the 135-degree point.)
* Reaching the 180-degree point with insufficient airspeed in a nose-high attitude. (Didn't release enough stick pressure back at the 45-degree point.)
* Reaching inconsistent altitudes at tops and bases. (Trouble lies in unequal pitch applications or incorrect power setting.)

In-flight Practice Guide

Pre-entry
* Minimum entry altitude: 2000 AGL.
* Clear for other traffic.
* Turn on landing light/strobes.
* Align with ground reference line.

Flying the Lazy Eight

Keypoint 1. * Apply pitch and bank simultaneously.
* Steadily increase back pressure and bank.

Keypoint 2. * Point of highest nose pitch.
* Start decreasing back pressure.
* Continue to increase bank.

Keypoint 3. * Lowest airspeed.
* Start decreasing bank.
* Continue to decrease back pressure.

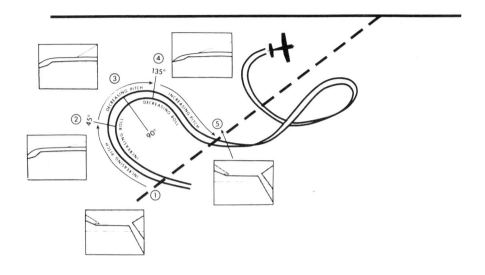

Keypoint 4.   * Point of lowest nose pitch.
                * Start increasing back pressure.
                * Continue to decrease bank.

Keypoint 5.   * Wings and nose pass through the level
                  attitude.
                * Climb and bank into the second half of
                  the lazy eight.
                * Repeat Keypoints 1–4 for second 180
                  degrees and recover on entry heading
                  to straight and level cruise.

Notes for Review

PYLON
EIGHTS

Pylon eights offer fast, close-packed action you seldom find in any other precision maneuver. This maneuver combines the finesse and self-discipline of the lazy eight with a dash of razzle-dazzle from aviation's golden age of pylon racing. It is easy to identify with the racing planes and pilots of the twenties and thirties as you turn your plane to pull tight around a pylon . . . visions of stubby, overpowered planes howling for position around the marked closed course . . . a whiff of hot engine oil . . . names like Gee Bee, The Laird Solution, and Jimmy Doolittle cross your mind.

But do not attempt the pylon eight until you have

proven yourself master of the load factors of the steep turn, the timing and coordination of the chandelle, and the orientation of the steep spiral. In pylon eights you fly *close* to the ground while you direct your attention outside of the cockpit. It is possible to let a skid force a high-speed stall . . . or to let a moment's unawareness fly you right into the ground. You need to *feel* this maneuver to fly it satisfactorily and safely. This is the primary purpose of the pylon eight—to evaluate and further develop a pilot's feel for aircraft control—his "feel for flying."

This feel for flying is something most pilots want to see in their own flying. Yet many find difficulty in achieving this feel—the instinct for flying. Usually a pilot experiences this difficulty simply because he does not know exactly what to look for. He does not have an *exact meaning* of the term "feel for flying"; an exact meaning that provides him with a goal for achievement.

So—let's list the specific factors that constitute the feel for flying, so we know exactly what we want to look for.

Feel for flying means:

1. You are aware of the aerodynamic forces that affect the airplane.
2. You are aware of the environment surrounding the airplane—the sight, sound, and feel that informs.
3. You anticipate the effects that the aerodynamic forces and the environment have on the plane, before those effects occur.

4. You compensate for the changing effects the instant they occur.
5. You know the limits of your airplane.

Consciously practice these five factors every moment you fly your plane. Before long, your conscious practice becomes subconscious aircraft control . . . and you find the "feel for flying." On takeoff, for example, your subconscious awareness of slipstream effect automatically causes you to apply a touch of right rudder against a crooked launch. As you rotate, your feel for flying anticipates the P-factor with a bit more rudder to prevent a swerve. And your awareness of the wind determines your actions in light of your plane's crosswind capability. Your crosswind correction goes into play even as your tires leave the ground for a climb-out straight along the centerline.

The feel for flying, then, is an awareness of forces and conditions that affect your airplane, and your compensation for those forces and conditions *before* they affect your plane adversely. It is the difference between *managing* a situation and *correcting* a situation.

Pylon eights provide an excellent opportunity for you to observe the development of your own "feel for flying." Your ability to anticipate the next moment and to react with precision is very visible to you during the maneuver. As we shall soon see, visual references readily seen throughout pylon eights give you a second-by-second evaluation of your ability to fly by instinct.

Pylon eights are also called "eights on pylons": a ground-reference maneuver in which the pilot flies a

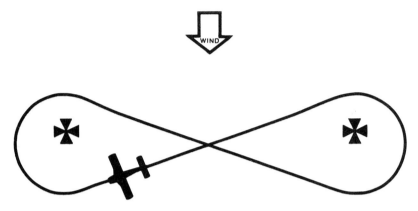

Figure 19
The pylon eight is a ground-reference maneuver that follows a figure-eight flight path around two pylons.

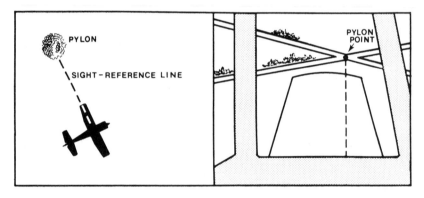

Figure 20
Your sight-reference line is a projection of your fixed line-of-sight reference, parallel to the plane's lateral axis.

figure eight around two "pylons" on the ground (Figure 19). You do *not* correct for wind drift, except between pylons. In fact, you just allow your plane to drift with the wind as you circle each pylon. The circles around the pylons, therefore, are not of a constant radius.

The objective is to fly the maneuver so that your *sight-reference line* remains fixed on each pylon as you circle it. (Sight-reference line is defined as a projection of a fixed line-of-sight reference, parallel to the plane's lateral axis, as depicted in Figure 20.)

Before you take the maneuver to the air, you should learn the relationship of the pivotal altitude to ground speed; the sight-reference line to pivotal altitude; and angle of bank to wind direction.

Relationship of the pivotal altitude to ground speed. For any given ground speed there is only *one* altitude that lets you keep your sight-reference line fixed on the pylon as you circle it. Your job is to capture and maintain this critical height, called the *pivotal altitude.* However, it varies as the wind varies the plane's ground speed (Figure 21). *The faster the ground speed, the higher the pivotal altitude; the slower the ground speed, the lower the pivotal altitude.* This fact is a function of motion and mathematics. Pivotal altitude equals ground speed squared, divided by 15. (Or as a mathematician would say:

$$PA = \frac{(V)^2}{15}.)$$

Thus, with any wind present, you vary your altitude as you circle the pylon. And since the wind constantly changes your ground speed around the pylon, your

Figure 21
The pivotal altitude varies as the wind varies your ground speed. The faster the ground speed, the higher the pivotal altitude. The slower the ground speed, the lower the pivotal altitude.

altitude constantly varies. But while the altitude corrections are continual, they are small. The overall altitude range circling a pylon is generally less than 75 feet. The pivotal altitude is a precise value; an error of only a few feet can cause you to lose hold of your sight-reference line to the pylon.

Relationship of the pilot's sight-reference line to the pivotal altitude. Your sight-reference line gives you a moment-to-moment evaluation of your ability to maintain a proper pivotal altitude as you circle the pylon. The apparent movement of the pylon, relative to your sight-reference line and wing tip, tells whether you are too high or too low for your ground speed. If the pylon appears to move forward of your sight-reference line, toward the leading edge of the wing tip, the plane is too high for its ground speed (Figure 22). Reduce altitude. If, on the other hand, the pylon seems to move behind your sight-reference line and toward the wing's trailing edge, raise your nose to maintain the pivotal altitude (Figure 23). *Pylon moving forward—go down; pylon moving rearward—pull up.*

Remember to keep your altitude adjustments *small,* because any you make has a dual effect: It will change both altitude *and* ground speed. Thus, a pylon that moves ahead of your sight-reference line tells you to adjust your altitude downward—your altitude is too high for your relatively slower ground speed (or, stated the other way, your ground speed is too slow for your altitude). When you lower your nose to correct your altitude, however, you also gain airspeed—which in turn increases your ground speed. The decreasing alti-

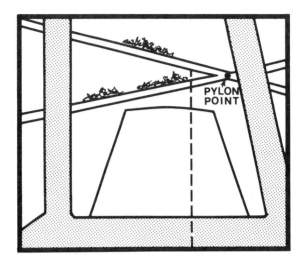

Figure 22
If the pylon appears to move forward of your sight-reference line, the plane is a few feet too high for the ground speed of the moment.

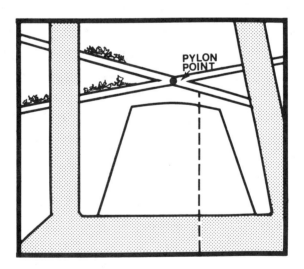

Figure 23
If the pylon seems to slip behind your sight-reference line, increase altitude slightly to maintain pivotal altitude.

tude and increasing ground speed combine to give your adjustment a dual role. (The reverse holds true when you adjust altitude upward.) You will find yourself successfully using small altitude adjustments *if* you anticipate the required adjustment of the next moment. Try to adjust your altitude one foot at a time, and the pylon will stay very near alignment with your sight-reference line.

Use your wing tip to establish an allowable tolerance for error in pivotal altitude. Keep the apparent movement of the pylon within the span of your wing tip. Give yourself a passing grade if you never let the pylon creep ahead of the wing tip's leading edge or slip behind the trailing edge. If you exceed these tolerances, break away from the pylon and reenter the maneuver, for it is useless to try and correct a large error with a large pitch-change. This changes the ground speed drastically, and you stand little chance of rematching altitude and ground speed.

Basically, you have a choice of ways in which to hold your pylons within the allowable range. You can make small corrections as small errors in altitude occur, or you can prevent any errors from occurring in the first place. Naturally, the latter method produces a smoother pylon eight. And it isn't too difficult to accomplish once you develop a *feel for the maneuver.* This *feel* can be discussed in specifics. First, you must understand the relationship between ground speed and pivotal altitude. Second, you must remain aware of the wind direction throughout the maneuver. Then you must constantly anticipate the effect the wind will have on your ground speed in the next moment. Finally, you must apply the anticipated altitude adjustment the instant before it is required. Thus, your feel for the maneuver is merely knowing the forces that effect your plane and then planning ahead to meet them.

Relationship of bank to wind direction. You do not vary your bank around the pylon to maintain a constant radius. Indeed, if any wind at all exists, your flight path around the pylon is asymmetrical, as in Figure 24.

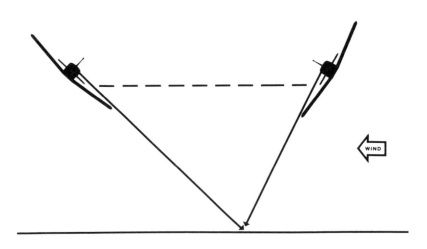

Figure 24
With any wind present, the radius of your turn around the pylon is asymmetrical. Just allow the plane to drift while you hold the pylon with the correct pivotal altitude.

Allow your plane to drift as you hold your pylon with the correct pivotal altitude.

You should vary your bank as you circle the pylon for quite another reason. Notice that there is a "vertical" space of several inches between the wing tip and the sight-reference line to the pylon. (In a low-winged aircraft, this space is above the wing tip; in a high-winged plane, the space is below the wing tip.) Vary your bank to maintain this space between the tip and your sight-reference line as you turn around the pylon. As the wind pushes you in toward the pylon, steepen your bank to maintain a constant space between wing tip and sight-reference line. And shallow your bank as the wind pushes you away from the pylon.

Here the function of pitch is to keep the sight-reference line constantly fixed on the pylon at pivotal altitude. The function of roll is to maintain a constant space between the sight-reference line and pylon.

Begin your in-flight practice of pylon eights with a drill that helps you to establish your sight-reference line, determine your plane's approximate pivotal altitude, and visualize the relationships between pivotal altitude and the apparent movement of the pylon against your sight-reference line. A drill in the form of a spiral descent over a single pylon accomplishes all three purposes. Start your spiral from an altitude considerably higher than your plane's average pivotal altitude (the average altitude is about 550 feet for a Cessna 152; 800 feet for a Cherokee). Fly at cruise speed in your spiral, the same speed you will use in the pylon eight.

From the moment you begin your spiral and until you descend to pivotal altitude, the pylon remains ahead of your sight-reference line. The pylon moves closer to alignment with your sight-reference line the closer you descend to the correct pivotal altitude, and you have the opportunity to take an unhurried look at the visual clue that tells you the plane is too high (pylon forward of wing tip).

Watch closely as the pylon moves into exact alignment with your sight-reference line. Quickly glance at your altimeter, because *that altitude* is your pivotal altitude (for the ground speed of the moment, of course).

Continue to spiral down slightly below pivotal altitude. The pylon slides behind your sight-reference line and you can see the visual reference that shows you are beneath the pivotal altitude.

The pivotal altitude that you determine from this drill is only approximate. It does not take into consideration that wind changes ground speed as you circle a pylon, nor the slight reduction in airspeed that occurs during the turns. The approximate pivotal altitude that you determine from this drill, though, is a good entry altitude for your maneuver.

Tackle pylon eights a step at a time. First, practice holding a pylon by flying around just one. Carefully select the single pylon for your first practice session, one with landmarks around it to help you keep track of the relative wind direction as you circle the point. A road intersection works fine; just be sure to clear the area for obstacles.

Enter the maneuver on the upwind side of your pylon so that you can roll into the steepest bank just as your sight-reference aligns with the pylon. Fly your pylons using a 30-degree bank. Pilots commonly tend to enter the turn too early. Delay your entry until you reach a point abeam the pylon (Figure 25). If you bank too soon, roll away momentarily from the pylon and then swing back into the turn when you reach the abeam position. If you fly slightly past that point, roll steeply into the pylon until you can fix your sight-reference line on it. And don't lean away from the turn; riding the plane sidesaddle renders your sight-reference line useless. (And good control coordina-

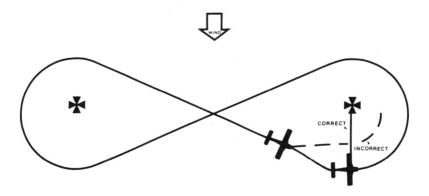

Figure 25
Do not enter your turn around the pylon too early; enter when you are *abeam* the pylon.

tion is virtually impossible if you don't sit properly.)

A pilot will often try to hold the pylon by the simple expedient of swinging his wing tip forward or rearward with the rudder. If the pylon slips behind his sight-reference line, for example, he uses bottom rudder in an attempt to swing the wing tip rearward. If the pylon creeps ahead of his reference line, he tries to swing the wing tip forward with top rudder. Of course, you cannot expect to hold the pylon by this method—and still have coordinated controls. Hold the pylon as you circle it *with variations in altitude*. Keep track of your wind, anticipate your ground speed for the next moment, and smoothly compensate with small variations in altitude.

Once you master turns on a single pylon, pick a suitable pair of pylons and expand your drill to the full pylon eight. If you fly a low performance trainer, select pylons about a half mile apart. Higher performance planes need pylons about three-fourths of a mile apart. These distances allow you a moment's straight and level flight between pylons. You have time to quickly evaluate your performance around the pylon that you just circled and to plan for the next one.

Try to use pylons that rest on equal ground elevations. Even a 15- or 20-foot difference makes it unnecessarily difficult to gauge the pivotal altitude. Use the bases rather than the tops of your pylons if trees or other landmarks of different height are chosen.

Road intersections make excellent pylons, particularly for the right-turn pylon, which is hidden from view at just the time you want to enter the turn around it. You can make good use of the intersection to estimate the position of the pylon itself.

Pick pylons that won't take you over any homes or livestock. The maneuver looks and sounds alarming when viewed from the ground by a nonpilot—so don't set the cause of aviation back twenty years in your own neighborhood. A review of Federal Aviation Regulation 91.79 (Minimum Safe Altitudes) is in order. It reads in part:

1. Over congested areas: 1000 feet above the highest obstacle within 2000 feet of your plane.
2. Over other areas: 500 feet above the surface.

You may find the maneuver easier to fly with pylons at right angles to the wind because similar crosswind corrections can be used when flying between the pylons. Try it, but you really should develop the ability to enter and fly the maneuver regardless of wind direction.

Before you enter pylon eights, practice-circle the first pylon to gauge the wind. Leave the pylon when your sight-reference line is abeam that pylon (Figure 26). Correct for the crosswind as you fly between the pylons so that your ground track brings you in proper position to tackle the other one. Fly the pylons with a maximum bank of 30 to 40 degrees.

Practice until you're good—really good. Then one day, when you need to relax, fly your plane out to your pylons. Hang on to stick and throttle. Screw down tight

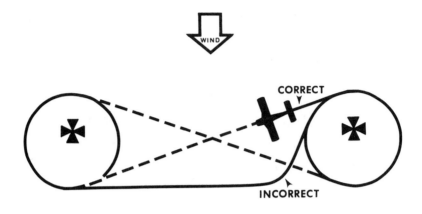

Figure 26
Leave the pylon when your sight-reference line is abeam that pylon.

into the seat, curl your toes around the rudder pedals, and swing the wing tip around those pylons. Work in the cockpit, quite alone, behind the singing engine . . . and grab yourself a slice of action from the golden age of aviation.

1 If your pylon appears to move ahead of your sight-reference line, you must descend slightly to capture the pivotal altitude for the ground speed of the moment.

2 You know that you are maintaining the pivotal altitude when you keep the pylon in alignment with your sight-reference line.

3 If the pylon appears to slip behind your sight-reference line, you are below the pivotal altitude and must climb slightly.

Preflight Review

The Maneuver
A ground track flown in a figure eight around two pylons while maintaining pivotal altitude.

Pilot Skill Developed
The ability to fly by instinct; the "feel for flying."

Performance Standards
Pivotal altitude: Pylon must remain within width of wing tip.

Bank: $\pm$ 10 degrees of that desired at the point of maximum roll.

Ground track: Straight between pylons.

Controls: Coordinated throughout.

Performance Tips
* Select pylons that lie perpendicular to the wind.
* Select pylons ½ mile apart for low performance aircraft; ¾ mile apart for higher performance planes.
* Pivotal altitude varies *constantly* around the pylon as the wind varies your ground speed.
* The faster your ground speed, the higher the pivotal altitude; the slower your ground speed, the lower your pivotal altitude.
* Use your sight-reference line to maintain the pivotal altitude.
* If the pylon moves forward of your sight-reference line, you are above the pivotal altitude for the ground speed of the moment—descend a few feet.

* If the pylon slips behind your sight-reference line, you are below the pivotal altitude for the ground speed of the moment—climb slightly.
* You are maintaining pivotal altitude when the pylon stays aligned with your sight-reference line.
* Pitch adjustments have a double value when you correct for pivotal altitude. They change both altitude *and* ground speed—so keep pitch changes small.
* *Anticipate* the needed corrections to your altitude; keep track of the wind direction.
* The "feel" of the pylon eight is merely knowing what conditions you must contend with, then planning ahead to deal with them as they occur.
* Practice the sight-reference technique by first working around a single pylon.

Common Mistakes

* Poor selection of pylons. (Pylons that lie along a road are easy to recognize during the fast action of pylon eights.)
* Entering the turn around the pylon too early. (Wait until your sight-reference line aligns itself with the pylon, the position abeam the pylon.)
* Leaning away from the turn. (Sit straight against the back of the seat.)
* Holding the pylon by swinging the wing tip forward or rearward with rudder. (A tough habit to break if you let it get started. Check the ball frequently to verify coordinated controls.)
* Over-controlling pitch to maintain the pivotal altitude. (Think in terms of changing your altitude one foot at a time.)

* Flying an inconsistent ground track between the pylons. (Make sure you *leave* a pylon only when abeam of it.)

In-flight Practice Guide

Pre-entry
* Clear for other traffic.
* Turn on landing light/strobes.
* Clear maneuver area for obstacles/population/livestock.
* Descend to approximate pivotal altitude (———— AGL).
* Set power for slower of cruise or maneuvering speed. (————RPM ————MP).

Flying the Pylon Eight
Keypoint 1. * Enter abeam first pylon.
      * Approximate pivotal altitude.
      * Power setting for entry speed.

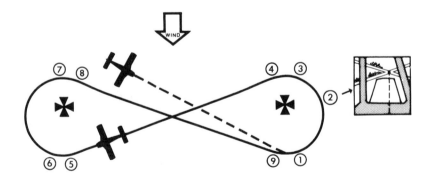

Keypoint 2. * Try to capture pivotal altitude.
* Pivotal altitude decreasing into the wind.

Keypoint 3. * Allow wind to drift plane toward pylon.
* Increase bank to maximum desired angle. (Maintain constant space between wing tip and sight-reference line.)

Keypoint 4. * Depart first pylon at abeam position.
* Correct for wind drift—fly a straight path to entry point of second pylon.

Keypoint 5. * Enter the turn around second pylon.
* Approximate pivotal altitude.

Keypoint 6. * Allow wind to drift plane away from pylon.
* Decrease bank to minimum angle to maintain constant space between wing tip and pylon.
* Try to capture pivotal altitude.
* Anticipate a reduction in pivotal altitude as you turn into wind.

Keypoint 7. * Increase bank to maximum angle desired.

Keypoint 8. * Depart second pylon.

Keypoint 9. * Either conclude maneuver or enter second pylon eight pattern. Recover on entry heading at straight-and-level cruise.

Notes for Review

PRECISION SLOW FLIGHT

Slow flight, by definition, is flying at any airspeed below normal cruise speed. An approach to a landing is a slow-flight maneuver. So is a climb. For our purposes, slow flight is a precision airspeed maneuver flown at three specific airspeeds:

Approach speed (1.3 × power-off, flaps-up stall speed—V_{SO}.)

10 knots (11.5 MPH) above approach speed

10 knots (11.5 MPH) below approach speed

Your slow-flight drills at each of these speeds in turn will use various flap settings while you maintain altitude, heading, and slow-flight airspeed.

First, the drills develop your instinctive ability to transition from cruise speed to a precise approach speed, without loss of altitude or heading. Second, they demonstrate the critical relationships between pitch, power, and change in flap settings. Finally, precision slow flight heightens your *feel* for precise trim control.

The built-in ability to move quickly and accurately from cruise to approach speed is a handy talent. If, for example, you need to allow spacing ahead of you in the landing pattern, just slow to approach speed smoothly and decisively. *And* when the time comes to set up your approach, half your work is done—your approach speed is already established.

An emergency go-around is often a critical slow-flight situation. You can fly according to the outside situation and not the panel *if,* through practice, you instinctively know how power, pitch, and flaps will interact.

Slow-flight practice teaches us that we must retrim with any change in power or flap setting, and do so in a moment's time, almost subconsciously. Develop your skill in slow flight so that you can fly the exercises while you maintain:

1. Airspeed within 5 knots of desired airspeed
2. Heading within 10 degrees of entry heading
3. Altitude within 100 feet of your entry altitude

4. Precise trim
5. Coordinated controls during entry, slow-flight drill, and recovery

Before you begin the actual slow-flight drills (and these should be flown at 2000 AGL minimum), take to the air and determine by trial and error the *pitch and power combinations that produce each of the three slow-flight speeds.* Changing quickly and easily to a precise slow airspeed is simply a matter of knowing how high to hold your plane's nose and how low to set the throttle. The exact pitch and power settings vary slightly for a given airspeed, even among planes of the same make and model. The condition of the plane, altitude, gross weight, and other factors make a precise pitch/power combination difficult to predict. But you can use a few rules of thumb:

1. 2000 RPM and a two-dot upward deflection on the attitude indicator will approximate approach speed ($1.3 \times V_{so}$) in fixed-pitch propeller aircraft.
2. The same two-dot deflection and 2000 RPM, with 20" manifold pressure, approximates approach speed in a variable-pitch propeller, single-engine aircraft. (Gear down if your plane is retractable.)
3. A 100 RPM (fixed pitch prop) or 1" MP (variable pitch prop) increase or decrease changes the airspeed 10 knots in the slow-flight speed range.
4. A one-half-dot deflection up or down moves the vertical-speed indicator needle 200 FPM.

Set up your trial pitch/power combination and wait for the airspeed to stabilize as you hold the VSI on zero with half-dot deflections. Once the speed is stable, note the airspeed indicated. And plan any power adjustment using rule-of-thumb number three above.

Of course, when you increase power, you must diminish pitch to prevent a climb (reduce your pitch a half-dot for each 100 RPM [or 1″ MP] increase). By the same token, a reduction in power calls for a pitch increase to prevent a descent. (Increase pitch a half-dot for each 100 RPM reduction.)

Also determine the *pitching moments caused by extending or retracting flaps.* Once you know the pitch/power combination needed to hold altitude at approach speed, lower the flaps one notch at a time—as you maintain approach speed. Chances are the existing power is adequate for the first notch of flaps, but your plane tends to rise. So lower the nose, trim forward. And note how much trim, and memorize the pitch attitude for approach speed with a single notch of flaps.

Then drop the second notch of flaps and watch the plane slow considerably and pitch upward. Add power (100 RPM per 10 knots), lower the nose farther, and retrim for the required power and pitch attitude. Note these as well.

Test the adjustments of pitch, power, and trim that each flap position requires. You may find that full-flaps at approach speed requires a decidedly nose-down attitude, high power, and considerable forward trim. You may also find yourself shoving a heavier and heavier right foot against torque as you slow-fly at higher power setting; it's needed to hold your heading and keep the ball centered.

After slow flight with full flaps, reverse the procedure. *Retract* the flaps one notch at a time. Reposition the nose to its proper pitch attitude as you move the flaps back to the previous setting. Reduce the power as required for each flap position and quickly retrim. Work swiftly with pitch, power, trim, and rudder. Anticipate pitch attitude, throttle setting, and trim for the next flap setting. Keep airspeed indicator, altimeter, heading indicator, and ball in their appointed places.

Finally, *analyze the relationship between slow flight and rate of turn.* Many pilots are caught unawares by the surprisingly rapid rates of turn in slow flight. Expect your plane's spinner to sweep the horizon fast in a normal turn in slow flight. *For any given angle of bank, the slower the airspeed, the faster the rate of turn.* Don't think you are doing something wrong when the plane turns on a dime. It's supposed to.

As you practice the drills, remember to watch your engine temperature, and be alert for head-on traffic lurking behind that upturned cowl.

PRACTICE GUIDE—PRECISION SLOW FLIGHT

Preflight Review

The Maneuver

A precision airspeed drill flown at three specific airspeeds: approach speed; 10 knots (11.5 MPH) above approach speed; 10 knots below approach speed.

Pilot Skills Developed

Airspeed control.

Precise trimming.

Coordinated pitch, power, and flaps.

Performance Standards

Altitude control: $\pm$ 100 feet.

Airspeed control: $\pm$ 5 knots (5.7 MPH).

Heading control: $\pm$ 10 degrees.

Performance Tips

* Use ground reference lines to help you: maintain a desired heading; effect recovery from the turning drills on the desired recovery heading.

* Torque effect will increase with reductions in airspeed and increases in power.

* Flap extensions or added power will tend to pitch the nose upward.

* Flap retractions or power reductions will tend to pitch the nose downward.

* Flap extensions will require increased power and lower nose to maintain a constant airspeed.

* A 100-RPM (fixed prop) or 1″ MP (constant-speed prop) change will increase or decrease the

airspeed about 10 knots (11.5 MPH) in the slow-flight speed range.

* A one-half-dot deflection on the attitude indicator will correct for 200 FPM climb or descent.
* You will experience a faster-than-expected rate of turn in your slow-flight turning drills.

Common Mistakes

* Not knowing where you must reposition the nose relative to the horizon as you change power or flaps. (Establish your visual references beforehand.)
* Allowing the torque to pull the plane off the desired heading. (Keep track of your ground reference line through the side window rather than out over the upturned nose.)
* Allowing excessive airspeed variations while changing power or flaps. (*Know* your visual pitch reference for each power/flap configuration. Move the nose to the required pitch attitude as you change the power and flaps.)
* Allowing the airspeed to diminish during the slow-flight turns. (Add an extra 50 RPM during the turns.)
* Losing altitude on the recovery. (Increase power to cruise as you *slowly* lower the nose.)

In-flight Practice Guide

Pre-entry
  * Minimum entry altitude: 2000 AGL.
  * Clear area for other traffic.
  * Turn on landing light/strobes.

Flying the Slow-Flight Drills

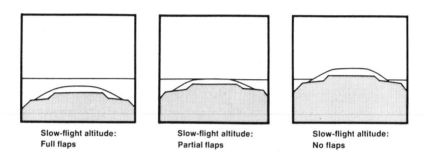

Slow-flight altitude: Slow-flight altitude: Slow-flight altitude:
Full flaps   Partial flaps   No flaps

Drill 1:   Fly the three slow-flight speeds within the performance standards.

Step 1. *Decelerate to approach speed plus 10 knots (11.5 MPH).* (To decelerate quickly, reduce power 300 RPM below that needed for slow flight.)

Step 2. *Lift nose as plane starts to settle.* (Watch the VSI or feel it in the seat of your pants.)

Step 3. *Increase the power for slow flight.* (As the plane decelerates to desired speed.)

Step 4. *Retrim.*

Step 5. *Decelerate to approach speed.* (Simultaneously raise nose and reduce power so airspeed and altitude remain constant.)

Step 6. *Retrim.*

Step 7. *Decelerate to approach speed minus 10 knots (11.5 MPH).* (Simultaneously readjust pitch and power.)

Step 8. *Retrim.*

Step 9. *Accelerate to approach speed.* (Simultaneously readjust pitch and power.)

Step 10. *Retrim.*

Step 11. *Accelerate to approach speed plus 10 knots (11.5 MPH).* (Simultaneously readjust pitch and power.)

Step 12. *Retrim.*

Step 13. *Return to cruise speed.* (Slowly lower the nose as you increase power to 100 RPM above cruise for a rapid speed recovery.)

Step 14. *Retrim for cruise flight.*

Drill 2: Repeat the fourteen steps of Drill #1 while you maintain a 30-degree banked 720-degree turn. (Establish initial slow-flight speed before entering turn.)

Drill 3: Use each available flap position, in turn, while you maintain straight and level flight at approach speed.

Step 1. *Decelerate to approach speed.*

Step 2. *Retrim.*

Step 3. *Lower first increment of flaps.* (Lower nose and add slight power.)

Step 4. *Retrim.*

Step 5. *Lower, in turn, each remaining flap increment.* (Lower nose and add power each time.)

Step 6. *Retrim after each flap and power change.*

Step 7. *Reduce flaps, one increment at a time, back to a clean wing.* (Simultaneously raise nose and reduce power with each flap change.)

Step 8. *Retrim after each flap and power change.*

Step 9. *Recover to straight and level cruise.*

Drill 4:   Repeat the nine steps of Drill #3 while you maintain a 30-degree banked 720-degree turn. (Establish slow-flight speed before entering turn.)

Notes for Review

ACCURACY LANDINGS

As a precision maneuver, an accuracy landing plants your tires on the runway on a point within 200 feet beyond your intended touchdown target. It's not hard to do if you follow a few tips.

First, fly a precise pattern. Keep your downwind leg half a mile from the runway, at pattern altitude, and a pattern speed of $1.7 \times$ stall (V_{SO}). A downwind leg half a mile from the runway is close enough to keep you from delaying other traffic, yet gives you adequate time to plan your approach. Keep your downwind leg parallel to the runway: Define the downwind leg's ground track by selecting landmarks to help visualize the parallel flight path. Then watch for any wind drift against your visualized line and immediately correct for it.

A pattern altitude of 800 AGL is suitable for most light aircraft (but you must abide by the established pattern altitude at your field). Allow yourself a 50-foot margin for error, but *begin* every approach to an accuracy landing from the same altitude.

A pattern speed of 1.7 × stall works well in most single-engine airplanes. This is slow enough to keep the Mooneys from running over the plane ahead, yet fast enough to keep the 152's from holding up the flow of traffic. Close to approach speed, it makes the transition to your landing-approach speed that much easier.

Begin the approach to your accuracy landing from the downwind leg, abeam your intended touchdown target. Select the second centerline stripe beyond the runway numbers as your target—with its midpoint as the bull's-eye. Centerline stripes are a standard 120 feet in length separated by 80 feet. Thus, if you touch down before the mid-point of the succeeding stripe, you are within the desired 200 feet of the bull's-eye. Choosing the second stripe as your target allows a safe margin for error in case of an undershoot. *Do not* use the runway numbers as your touchdown target. (Frankly, pilots who turn to me in the cockpit and announce that they are "gonna plant it on the number" start me squirming in the seat.)

Abeam position, reduce power to 1700 RPM (or 17″ MP) and trim to an approach speed of 1.3 × stall. This power setting permits a manageable descent in most

light planes and only minor adjustments during the
letdown are needed. A *partial* power descent has three
advantages over a power-off approach:

1. Your engine responds quicker to a power increase that
   might be needed to correct for a low glide path.
2. You have greater flexibility. With partial power you can
   either increase it or decrease it. On a power-off approach
   you can only increase it.
3. A power-off approach causes an excessive sink rate; partial
   power keeps sink in hand.

If you slow to approach speed early enough in the
approach, you'll avoid trouble. The activities of the approach and landing come at you faster than you can
sort them out. Slow to approach speed *before* you turn
base leg, and the approach will unfold before you in
seemingly slow motion.

Plan your approach with partial flaps rather than full
flaps. This gives your landing descent greater flexibility.
If, for example, you see on short final that you are
overshooting, you will still have additional flaps in reserve with which to shorten the approach. On the other
hand, if you are undershooting, you will need a smaller
power increase than would have been required with
flaps fully extended. Large power changes on final can
drastically affect an approach; they often make for a
poor landing.

An approach flown with partial flaps offers advantages over one flown with flaps up. With flaps already
partially extended, the glide path immediately steepens with the application of additional flaps. The air-

plane's response to flaps is not as rapid if the flaps are extended from the completely retracted position. Flaps also increase the margin between stalling speed and approach speed, adding a safety factor to the landing descent.

On base leg, plan your turn to final at an altitude that helps assure an accurate touchdown. You can easily do this if you pick a landmark on final, one-half mile out from your touchdown target. Let that landmark serve as a final approach fix. Here is how it works:

Reduce your power on the downwind leg, opposite your touchdown target, at 800 AGL (assuming 800 AGL is pattern altitude). Now your goal is to gauge your descent so that you cross your final-fix landmark at 400 AGL. After you turn base leg (you are now at about 700 AGL), eyeball the distance remaining to the half-mile landmark against the altitude that you have yet to lose in order to cross your final fix at 400 AGL. If you think you are too low, add 100 RPM. If you are too high, reduce power by 100 RPM. Then reevaluate your *altitude to lose* versus *distance to travel,* at each 50 feet of altitude lost. Make 100 RPM power changes accordingly as you descend toward the final-fix landmark. Make frequent reevaluations and small power adjustments to assure a turn to final that allows you to cross your fix at 400 AGL, half a mile out. The point is this—the half-mile reference point gives you an intermediate altitude objective. Without this it is difficult to manage your descent throughout the entire approach involving two changes in direction.

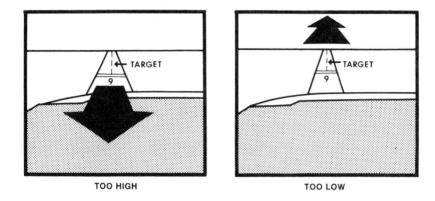

Figure 27
If you are high, the target appears to move downward and toward you. If you are low, your target appears to move upward and away.

Look for traffic, turn to final over your fix, and lock your eyes on the touchdown target. Look for the *apparent movement* of the target. The apparent-movement method almost guarantees a touchdown on target. If your target appears to move upward or away, you will land short (Figure 27). If the target appears to move downward toward you, you will land long. If the target appears to remain motionless, however, you will touch down nearly on target. (Actually, you land slightly beyond the target as your glide path flattens out close to the ground. For a perfect bull's-eye, allow for this slight overshoot.) From the final approach fix to touchdown, change your power in small 100-RPM increments to hold your target motionless. Power changes greater than 100 RPM drastically alter your glide path and make an accurate touchdown impossible. Touch down with a normal correction for any crosswind.

Use either *stop-and-go* landings or *full-stop* landings in your practice. Avoid *touch-and-go* landings. With stop-and-go landings you come to a complete stop on the runway, tend to your cockpit chores, and take off again. With full-stop landings you of course clear the runway and taxi back for the next takeoff. In either case you devote your entire attention to your landing and roll-out. You do not have to think about the ensuing takeoff while you are busy landing. Stop-and-go or full-stop landings (if your runway is short) give you time in which to retract your flaps, retrim for takeoff, and close your carburetor heat while your plane is stopped. On touch-and-go landings you have to perform these tasks while you roll pell-mell down the runway. A complete stop also gives you the chance to reposition your plane astride the centerline, if necessary, and plan an orderly takeoff. Touch-and-go landings sometimes fling you into the air from the edge of the runway.

It is argued that touch-and-go landings save time and money. They may, but they also teach poor habits and improper procedures.

Once you are satisfied with your accuracy landings, use this technique to conclude every flight. Try to make *all* your landings accuracy landings. You may miss your touchdown target, but your efforts toward accuracy will reward you with a smooth landing—far smoother than an approach to land "somewhere in the first third of the runway." It is the difference between a halfhearted effort and a 100 percent effort—and that's *all* the difference.

PRACTICE GUIDE—ACCURACY LANDINGS

Preflight Review

The Maneuver
A precision landing that plants your tires where you intend to touch down.

Pilot Skills Developed
Advance planning of pattern and approach. Landing technique under adverse conditions.

Performance Standards
Touch down in a normal landing attitude astride the centerline, on the target or within 200 feet beyond.

Performance Tips
* A good landing starts with a precise pattern. Fly an accurate pattern altitude and correct for any drift.
* Let the midpoint of a centerline stripe serve as your touchdown target. If you land before reaching the mid-point of the succeeding stripe, you have touched down within acceptable performance standards.
* Plan to fly your approach with partial flaps.
* Adjust power on final to compensate for the *apparent motion* of your touchdown target: Target moving upward or away from you—add power; target moving downward or toward you—reduce power.

Common Mistakes
* Flying inconsistent patterns. (Use ground refer-

ence points to help visualize the downwind and
base legs.)
* Arriving over the half-mile final-fix landmark too
high or too low. (Reevaluate your *altitude to lose*
versus *distance to fly* at each 50 feet of altitude
lost, after turning to the base leg.)
* Making a last-second bid with a large power adjustment on short final. (Learn to detect the
need for a power change early on final. Then
make a small power adjustment.)

In-flight Practice Guide

Pre-entry
* Establish pattern altitude on the downwind leg,
half a mile from runway.

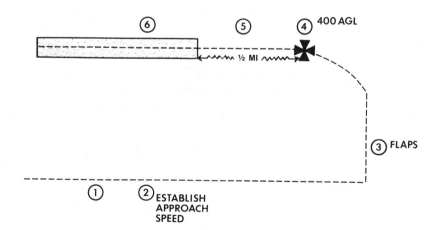

* Clear for other traffic.
* Turn on landing light/strobes.
* Select a highly visible landmark to identify the half-mile final-approach fix.
* Choose the second centerline stripe midpoint as your touchdown target.

Flying the Accuracy Landing

Keypoint 1. * Establish the downwind leg at normal pattern speed.
            * Establish a wind correction angle to prevent wind drift.

Keypoint 2. * Reduce power to 1700 RPM.
            * Establish approach speed before turning base.
            * Retrim.

Keypoint 3. * Evaluate distance to final-approach fix versus altitude to lose.
            * Extend partial flaps.
            * Retrim.

Keypoint 4. * Cross fix at 400 AGL.
            * Look for apparent motion of touchdown target.

Keypoint 5. * Hold touchdown target motionless with small throttle movements.
            * Retrim for each power change.

Keypoint 6. * Evaluate any overshoot or undershoot to improve the next attempt.
            * Roll out to full stop.

Notes for Review

SHORT-FIELD LANDINGS

This chapter treats the *short-field landing* as a precision maneuver rather than an exercise in operational training. The simulated short-field landing drill that we undertake here deals with the flying required to descend over a 50-foot obstacle and land safely within the shortest possible ground roll. Our precision drill does not consider the operational aspects of actually getting a plane safely into a short strip. Runway slope, density altitude, turbulence, wet grass, hazardous approaches, go-arounds, and other operational considerations are subjects in themselves.

Before you begin in-flight practice, decide how much

usable runway to allow yourself for satisfactory performance of the precision short-field landing. Refer to the landing charts in your aircraft operations manual. These charts will help you calculate how the variables of field elevation, temperature, head wind, and aircraft weight affect the landing distance on a paved runway.

Determine the minimum runway needed for the conditions surrounding your flight. Obtain the field elevation from your sectional chart. Look to your outside air-temperature gauge, and work out your head-wind component from the wind sock. (A wind sock stiffens at 15 knots. If it is hanging at a 45-degree angle, the wind is about 8 knots. If the sock is swinging within 30 degrees of runway alignment, consider all wind velocity as a head-wind component. If the sock is blowing from 30 to 60 degrees off the runway, figure the head-wind component at one-half the wind's velocity. And if the wind is blowing from 60 to 90 degrees across the runway, do not allow for any head-wind component.)

Calculate the distance required to clear a 50-foot obstacle, but remember that the landing chart assumes *average pilot ability.* And your performance must be above average. So take this calculated distance and subtract 10 percent for *your* short-field landing.

Fly your plane to the downwind leg of a long paved runway and visualize how much of that runway constitutes your simulated short field. Place your imaginary obstacle at the end of the runway and estimate your required distance by counting the runway boundary lights. They are a standard 200 feet apart. (Or count the runway center stripes—120 feet long, 80 feet apart.)

The approach to a simulated short field must achieve a steep descent to the landing and the slowest possible ground speed at touchdown. A steep descent permits you to clear the obstacle and still touch down close to the beginning of the runway. A slow touchdown speed enables you to stop the airplane within the shortest possible ground roll.

Achieve your steep descent by starting a power reduction immediately after crossing your simulated obstacle. Reduce power at a smooth rate that reaches idle throttle just as the tires touch. (Don't completely close the throttle as you cross the obstacle. While this method produces the very steepest descent, it also invites a damaged landing gear through an excessive rate of sink.)

Use full flaps to ensure the slowest possible ground speed. Most pilots find it better to apply half flaps on base leg and extend full flaps after turning final. Also, a slightly longer final gives extra time to establish and evaluate a proper glide path. Your glide path must clear your imaginary 50-foot obstacle by a 50-foot margin, yet be low enough for you to land reasonably close to the approach end of the runway.

Even though you fly a longer final leg, do use a half-mile-out reference point—as in accuracy landings. Plan your approach so that you cross this point at 400 AGL with full flaps extended, and at a speed equal to 1.3 × the *full-flap stall speed (V$_{SO}$)*. To cross your final-fix point at 400 feet, carry a little more power (about 200

RPM) than you use in an accuracy landing. You need this to adjust the steep glide path produced by full flaps and to compensate for the longer final leg.

After you cross the final-fix point, manage your descent to cross the imaginary obstacle by a 50-foot margin. Avoid large power adjustments after you pass your final-fix point; adjust power in 100-RPM stages. Larger increases or reductions in power throw your timing off.

After you cross the simulated obstacle, start a slow power reduction that has the throttle closed just as the tires touch.

If you fly a fixed-gear airplane, retract the flaps right after touchdown for better braking action. But if you fly a retractable, leave the flaps down. (Don't reach for a handle or switch until your plane is stopped and you can look down to be sure of the right knob.)

When can you use short-field technique on a long paved runway? When the controller tells you to land and hold short of the intersecting runway. Or when you land behind a departing jet; you want to be stopped before reaching his lift-off point, to avoid wake turbulence.

PRACTICE GUIDE—SHORT-FIELD LANDINGS

Preflight Review

The Maneuver

A procedure that safely lands the plane over a 50-foot obstacle within the shortest possible distance.

Pilot Skills Developed

The ability to make your plane do just what you intend it to do.

Performance Standards

Obstacle clearance: Within 50 feet above a 50-foot obstacle.

Landing distance: Within 90 percent of the calculated distance given by the airplane's landing charts.

Pilot technique: Smooth use of controls, power, brakes.

Performance Tips

* Visualize usable length of simulated short runway by counting runway center stripes. (120 feet long, 80 feet apart.)
* Short-field approach demands: a steep descent to touchdown; a slow ground-speed at touchdown.
* A power reduction after crossing the obstacle produces a steep descent.
* Full flaps allow slow forward speed.

Common Mistakes

* Rushing the approach and letting the plane get ahead of the pilot. (Fly a slightly wider base and longer final than normal.)

* Chopping the power after crossing the obstacle. (This will cause a hard landing.)

In-flight Practice Guide

Pre-entry
* Calculate required runway length from the plane's landing chart.
* Establish pattern altitude downwind, fly a slightly wider-than-normal pattern.
* Clear for other traffic.
* Turn on landing lights/strobes.
* Select a half-mile final-approach fix.
* Visualize the simulated 50-foot obstacle at the approach end on runway.
* Determine a landmark on the runway to represent the end of your simulated short runway.

Flying the Short-Field Landing

Keypoint 1. * Cross half-mile final-fix at 400 AGL.
* Full flaps.
* 1.3 × full-flap stall speed.

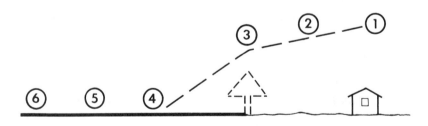

Keypoint 2.　* Evaluate rate of descent to proper height over obstacle.

　　　　　　* Use small power adjustments.

Keypoint 3.　* Clear obstacle by 50-foot margin. (Field elevation, plus 50-foot margin.)

　　　　　　* Start smooth power reduction.

Keypoint 4.　* Power reaches idle at touch down.

Keypoint 5.　* Retract flaps (fixed-gear aircraft).

　　　　　　* Apply smooth braking.

Keypoint 6.　* Stop airplane.

　　　　　　* Retract flaps (retractable-gear aircraft).

　　　　　　* Evaluate actual stopping distance.

　　　　　　* Reposition flaps, carburetor heat, trim, for next takeoff.

Notes for Review

CONCLUSION: PRECISION IN EVERY FLIGHT

Flying skills either improve or deteriorate, but they do not remain unchanged. I firmly believe that you *can* prevent deterioration of the skills you have developed in these maneuvers by striving for this same precision in *every* flight you make. And one day you will realize that you have captured it . . . your conscious effort toward perfection becomes subconscious habit.

How is the precision that the maneuvers demanded carried over to your everyday flying? Here are a few examples:

Takeoff   Begin every takeoff run exactly astride the centerline. Do not let slipstream swerve your initial roll or let P-factor spoil your lift-off. Be aware of any cross-wind and compensate *before* you drift; climb out directly over the centerline.

Maintain the exact climb-power setting recommended in your plane's operating manual—and the manufacturer's recommended climb speed within a 3-knot tolerance. Keep the ball centered as you climb out and leave the pattern.

Level-off   Begin your level-off to cruising altitude just before reaching it. Lead the level-off by 50 feet for each 500 FPM rate of climb. Level the nose slowly, with the engine still at climb power. Keep the ball centered as the plane quickly accelerates. Reduce the throttle to cruise power as your plane reaches cruise airspeed. You should level off within 20 feet of your desired altitude.

Cruise Flight   Straight and level flight is a precision maneuver—if you make it so. Trim your plane and adjust power with the accuracy that keeps you at your altitude within 20 feet. (It is easier to fly within a 20-foot tolerance than a 100-foot tolerance; it is easier to correct a 20-foot error than a 100-foot error.)

Hold your compass heading within 5 degrees. This is not a difficult standard to meet, with a rapid cross-check between your outside references and your panel. An accurately held heading offers a bonus to an exacting pilot—he usually knows right where he is. Pilots usually get lost through inattention to the heading their plane is flying.

Descent to Destination   Plan it as a precision VFR letdown. Begin when you are ten minutes out (in a 152, that's about 15 miles; in a Cherokee, 20 miles; in a Mooney, 30 miles). Decide how much altitude you must lose from your cruising level to the pattern altitude. If you are cruising at 5500 feet, and the pattern altitude ahead is 1500 feet, you have 4000 feet to lose in ten minutes. Simply lower your plane's nose slowly until the VSI needle rests on 400 FPM. The engine will over-rev as you head downhill, so ease the throttle back to stay at cruise power.

You gain efficiency as you pick up an extra 5 knots for each 200 FPM of descent. But of greater importance, you are planning ahead and flying with precision.

Correct . . . exact . . . precise: Is the pursuit worth the effort? Yes. Can you attain the goal? Yes—with constant and conscious effort. Deliberately try for perfection every moment you are in the cockpit. One day the conscious effort of precision flying is suddenly a habit as natural as fastening your seat belt. And you know that should you need it, you are ready with your *reserve of competence.*

A REWARDING "GRADUATION" FLIGHT

After you perfect your maneuvers, fly your last practice session with a friend aboard. Blend your maneuvers to give him an inside view of precision flying. Climb to 3000 feet and get set to show your best.

Roll the plane into a 50-degree left steep turn and

pour in power. Ease back on the stick to keep the nose level and pull the plane twice around the horizon. Then throttle the engine and roll into the right steep turn. Twice around once more while the G's press you tight against the seat.

Roll out of the turn and keep the wings rolling into a gentle left bank as you lift your plane's nose into the natural grace of a lazy eight. Lift the cowl higher . . . higher, to leave Earth far behind. Hang momentarily in space as the wings bank gently across the top of the eight. Then slice the spinner down through the horizon and feel the controls stiffen as your plane dives to the base of the maneuver. Roll through at the bottom and fly upward into the second half of your lazy eight. Over the top again with sagging ailerons and down the slope once more behind your singing engine . . . viewed from the cockpit, the eight is beautiful.

From your lazy eight fly directly upward into the chandelle's satin-smooth climbing turn. Stay nimble with rudder. Don't spoil the symmetry of the turn with a slip or skid. Fly with precision. Perform to the very best of your ability, so that your banked wings and silver-toned engine say to your friend: "This is *flying*— at its best."

Chandelle up in the opposite direction. Wait until the airspeed slows at the top. Then steepen your wings to a 50-degree bank, idle your engine, and ease the nose forward into a steep spiral. Spiral downward behind the whispering engine. Level at 1500 feet and turn for home—satisfied with a flight well flown.

AEROBATIC FLYING

Any pilot who learns to fly these precision maneuvers within the stated tolerances is ready to begin aerobatic training. The ability to loop, slow roll, split-S, or Immelmann is within your grasp—with competent instruction in the right airplane.

Aerobatic flying demands that you fly the plane and yourself even *closer* to the edge of its operating limits. In the interest of your own safety, be very careful in your choice of instructor and airplane. Has the instructor a background of aerobatic teaching? Do his students recommend him wholeheartedly? Is the airplane approved for aerobatics? And is it well maintained? If so —start training. You are prepared to reach beyond the realm of this book.